ARISE, SHINE, AND BE REVEALED

Miranda de Bruin

Edited by Chelsea Slade
Cover design by Bernard Dijkstra

ISBN: 1536843113
ISBN 13: 9781536843118

www.HuubandMiranda.com

CONTENTS

DEDICATION

I dedicate this book to Jesus, to the church—the whole body of Christ—His glorious sons and daughters, especially to my readers. It is my hope that as you read this book you would encounter Him—who He is and His heart for you. May you discover the dreams and passions He placed inside of you as you come fully alive and operate in your fullness, shining bright with all the beauty and glory of who He created you to be.
And may you fall in love again and again with our heavenly Father and who He is revealing Himself to be to you.

TESTIMONIES

Our heavenly Father, who loves each one so uniquely with immeasurable favor, is bursting with pride over this work. If ever there were a book written for His bride that would settle issues that divide us, this is that book! His love is so securing, so personal with revelation for our journey. In seeing Him clearly, how could we not see ourselves and our neighbor through His gaze. It changes everything! Arise, Shine, and Be Revealed articulates the beauty of walking in this reality and the reality of Christ in you, bringing heaven to earth. The intimacy Miranda has with our heavenly Father will inspire you as deep calls unto to deep. The questions posed in the chapters, facilitated a renewed and deeper intimacy in my conversations with the Father. They sparked dreams and prophetic visions of His abilities inside of me and His body as a whole. This is a book I will highly recommend to everyone I know. It is a book I will pull down and re-read many times over my life-time, and find new encouragement with each read. It is wealthy with prophetic insight and deliberate with practical applications. Arise, Shine and Be Revealed is powerful in its purpose to come alongside the Father and birth a work He is dreaming over us, His beloved ones!

Aimee Perry
Children's Pastor
King's Way Church
Birmingham, Alabama

ENDORSEMENTS

"In her new book, 'Arise, Shine, and Be Revealed,' Miranda de Bruin asks "why is it taking so long to spread God's kingdom into every corner of the earth?" This is an important question and she has some important answers. This book is filled with insights and nuggets of wisdom, you will be blessed!

Dr. Jonathan Welton
Best-Selling Author and President of Welton Academy

What a lovely book! ***Arise, Shine, and Be Revealed***, by Miranda De Bruin, is a book that was born out of great passion. I've known Miranda for years, and she has always carried within her a passionate desire for believers to see their Father for who He is, understand from that vantage point who they are, and then with confidence, boldly walk out their call. Every page reveals words that drip with sincerity and authenticity. So as the book declares, Arise in understanding, Shine in the light of that knowledge, and then let His light be revealed in you and through you to a world in need.

Chris DuPré
Associate Pastor, Life Center Church, Harrisburg, PA
Author of The Wild Love of God, and The Love Project

We consider it a great honor to have walked alongside, and to call Miranda a friend of our family. We have seen the fruit of this "Arise, Shine, and be Revealed" revelation alive and active in Miranda since we first met her, and have seen its incredible impact on others around her. We are living in a time where we as His body have an opportunity. We can succumb to fear in the midst of darkness and calamity, or radiate the incredible beauty of Christ... even in the midst of crisis. It's interesting that no matter how dark a room is, when the light switch is flipped to on, darkness has no options but to flee as light fills the room. We believe this book is the hand that flips that very switch on in each and every person that reads it. It's time for His sons and daughters to shine forth in all that He has planned and purposed for such a time as this. Our heart cry is the prayer of the Moravians...May the Lamb of God receive the reward of His suffering. You, my friend, are His reward. Arise and shine!!

Jeff and Suzanne Whatley
Associate and Worship Pastors
King's Way Church
Birmingham, Alabama

Arise, Shine, and Be Revealed is a beautifully written, vulnerable and authentic book. Miranda has exceptional revelation she has walked through with God and brings you into encounters of His heart for you, discovering the gifts, talents He placed inside of you. Empowering you to recognize Gods voice for yourself and others. It is supernatural, yet very practical. You will be changed after reading this book!

Tim and Sue Eldridge
Directors of Presence Ministries International
Harrogate, England

Miranda and her husband Huub have been dear friends for many years. I have watched her as she has lived out the very things she writes about in her book and can attest that both she and what she writes about are both her passion and deep in the heart of Father God. You will be inspired and changed as you read the insights and wisdom she brings.

Andy Reese
Author of Freedom Tools and Bleats
Franklin, TN

FOREWORD

ARISE!

Wow...what a read!
Such an intense breath of passion about the Father's love for people.

And this is exactly how I know Miranda and her husband Huub.
What she is writing is what I recognize in her life.
As she wrote: 'I live to impact peoples lives...to see people's lives restored'.

In this book she takes you by example and glimpses of her own life on a journey to discover, to see and to participate in the Father's dream for your life.

Miranda is relentless in her pursuit to let others know their value! The value which comes from the Fathers dream over peoples life.

This book is an invitation to encounter the Father of life.
It is to encourage you as reader to have vision for your life by exposure of the divine, to see, to hear and therefore to pursue your dreams and passions!

So beautiful as she wrote:
'As we see Him in His fullness, we see ourselves in our fullness.'

It is about the authority to become!
Yes, we become what we behold!

An invitation for all of us, to hear that passionate heart cry from the Father for us! To see, to dream, to know...

Be inspired as you read, 'to become what you behold'!

And yes, as glorious sons of the Father, you, I, we all, will SHINE!

Gerard Keurentjes
Senior Pastor
Eldad
Ede, The Netherlands

INTRODUCTION

Have you ever wondered why it is taking so long for the church to impact the world when there are so many churches and so many Christians? What are those things that keep us from advancing? Have you had times where you compared yourself to others—looked at others and thought they were more powerful or significant than you? Have you had a hard time hearing the voice of God or wanted to know how to operate in spiritual gifts? I'm very happy you picked up this book! I wrote this book especially for you, and it is my joy to take you on a journey of discovery, full of encounters and God's heart for you.

As we journey through this book, there will be times when you are prompted to dream with your heavenly Father. I will ask you questions throughout each chapter, and I encourage you to write down your responses. This is an interactive book, an invitation to process what you are discovering and come to your own conclusions and revelations.

Don't be discouraged if you feel like you have a hard time hearing from God. When you are prompted to listen for God's voice, write down the first thing that comes to your mind. What do you sense, feel, hear, or see? Write it down or maybe even draw it out.

After you've written or drawn it, then you can examine it and see if it was from Him. I go into greater detail of how to do this in the book.

This book is designed to activate you to:

- Discover the unique gifts you carry, the importance of those gifts, and how to release them into the world around you.
- Destroy the enemies of this great movement, which are competition and comparison, to name a few.
- Experience your significance, empowerment, and celebration.
- Encounter your heavenly Father—who He is and His heart for you.
- Live in victory over the enemy
- Recognize God's voice for yourself and others.
- Operate in spiritual gifts.

For years I wrestled with the questions of why it is taking us so long to make an impact on the world, and I wondered to myself, *what are we missing?* If we are all about advancing His kingdom, why are we not recognizing that we are on the same team? I am convinced that together we can have the greatest impact. I invite you to reap the fruit of what I have passionately pursued: to encourage you and empower you to come to your fullness.

It is my prayer and great desire that as you read this book, the Holy Spirit would hover over you and the very essence of who you are. May you realize that who you are, and the unique gifts and talents you carry, is great, valuable, and necessary. I pray you continually encounter His heart for you and the truth that He knows you, He is in every detail of your life, and He cares for you.

Let us begin our journey together, discovering God's vision and dream for us—His glorious sons and daughters!

CHAPTER 1
ARISE AND SHINE

You were created to be great! Everyone is created to be great and to fulfill a unique purpose and destiny. Your life is no accident. Your heavenly Father celebrated the day you were born. He dreamed over you and invested in you—your character, gifts, talents, and passions—so that you would be His dream come true on the earth and would live out your full potential. His heart is for all of His sons and daughters to live out all of the dreams, passions, and desires He placed in us, arising, shining, and revealing who He is and who we are to the world around us.

How do we define what it means to be great? What does the greatness you carry look like? And how do you activate it? Let me take you on a journey to discover the gifts, talents, and your unique heavenly expression on this earth. My goal on this journey is to empower you to arise and shine: to define, or redefine, what success and greatness look like and how it will practically play out in your life. The Father has a dream, and it's you! I pray that you hear and experience His dream over your life as we embark on our journey together.

The Vision

For years I wrestled intensely within myself with the questions such as, *Why is it taking us so long to make an impact on the world? There are so many churches, so many Christians—what is holding us back? How can we have an even greater impact?* The Father was highlighting and magnifying things to me that were going on inside the body of Christ around the world, things that were holding us back. It was confrontational and uncomfortable to see. However, I burned with passion to see a change. As uncomfortable and confrontational as it was, He said to me, "Embrace it." As I did, I cried out to Him with everything within me, and He gave me wisdom and revelation to empower the body of Christ. One of the things He showed me was His dream and vision for the church.

In 2012, The Father gave me a vision. I saw glory covering the earth in the form of this powerful and beautiful, bright shining light—shining bright like the sun. I saw that this glory was His sons and daughters, rising and shining in every realm of influence. And I heard the scriptures "Arise, shine, for your light has come, and the glory of the Lord rises upon you" (Isa. 60:1, NIV), and "For the earth will be filled with the knowledge of the glory of the Lord as the waters cover the sea" (Hab. 2:14, NIV). Captivated by what He was showing me, I realized this must be a visual representation of those verses. His sons and daughters are the great, bright shining lights of His glory covering the earth—consuming, covering, filling the world with His glory and goodness. They are shining bright with the knowledge of His glory in the world around them, expressing and revealing who He is.

His presence had an intense impact on my eyes, like an extreme heat that both branded and captivated me. For weeks, every time I worshipped I would feel an intense heat burning over my eyes. It was His presence washing, refining, and removing any judgment or criticism from my eyes. When I would enter His manifest presence, the vision would play again; I could sense His heartbeat—relentless and beautiful—for His dream to come true. I couldn't escape it, nor did I want to. I started seeing people in a new way. I could sense the Father's delight over His sons and daughters more than ever before, seeing the unique gifts He placed in them. I also began to realize that this is what I am living for—to see His sons and daughters arise, shine, and be revealed.

After He showed me the vision, I began to encounter His heart and thoughts for people with great delight. I've never thought of myself as a critical or judgmental person. However, sometimes we don't know there's more freedom until we become more free. As I encountered people differently, I realized that enjoying His thoughts and His heart for people and seeing them for who they really are is so much better, more fun, and full of life. What a better way to live—so much better than being irritated or negative. Thankfully, I became freer; I hadn't known all that I was missing out on.

Encountering people in this new way was sometimes like having an intense encounter with Jesus, being moved with the love and delight He had for each person. I would encounter His dreams, thoughts, and plans for each individual and experience thankfulness for what He placed inside of each person. I saw His value for them, and I became convinced that each person He revealed to me was needed and necessary. I would earnestly pray over them that everything He invested in them would come alive and be fully lived out.

People would sometimes pray over me, "Let all your dreams and visions in life come to pass!" I would become overwhelmed with great delight and joy in His presence. You are my dream! You are my vision!

That you would come to your fullness! That you would encounter His heart for you and enjoy the delight of His face. This is what I live for: that you, His sons and daughters, would arise, shine, and be revealed!

As you read this, I pray the same encounter for you: that His overwhelming presence would come upon you, His refining fire would wash over you and remove from your eyes any judgment or criticism. I pray that you would encounter His heart, thoughts, delight, and dreams for the people around you. And as you encounter people in a new way, enjoy being a releaser of His heart, promises, and truth, calling out the dream He had over them from the beginning. Isn't this a much better way to live?

In the same way, let the refiner's fire of love come and wash from your eyes any judgement or critism you've had over yourself. Let it continue until you become the very image He dreamed you to be from the beginning, seeing yourself for who you truly are.

Arise and Shine

> Arise, shine; for your light has come,
> And the glory of the Lᴏʀᴅ has risen upon you.
> For behold, darkness will cover the earth
> And deep darkness the peoples;
> **But** the Lᴏʀᴅ will rise upon you
> And His glory will appear upon you.
> Nations will come to your light,
> And kings to the brightness of your rising.

(Isa. 60:1–3, NIV)

Arise, from any depression in which circumstances have kept you. Arise to your new life in Christ. Shine and be radiant! The glory of the Lord has risen upon you. He placed His glory inside of you and you carry a unique, heavenly expression on this earth. And that unique expression needs to be seen and heard. You are full of wisdom, solutions, and revelation. You are a gateway—a portal to heaven wherever you go. You have the ability to connect with your heavenly Father and receive wisdom, solutions, and revelation. Wherever you are, His glory shall be seen in you, and "nations shall come to your light and kings to the brightness of your rising."

The world is waiting for you to arise and to be revealed. They are waiting for you to reveal the great glory that God has placed in you. Just as darkness disappears when a light is turned on, the darkness that has held people captive will flee as you arise and shine. Nations, kings, and people of influence will be drawn to the glory you carry. The only places where darkness can remain are the parts of the world where His sons and daughters have not arisen, where we haven't taken our position. Those are the darkest places, but we can eradicate darkness by arising and shining.

Filling the Earth

> For the earth will be filled with the knowledge of the glory
> of the LORD as the waters cover the sea.
>
> (Hab. 2:14, NIV)

What is the knowledge of His glory that will fill the earth? It is not mere head knowledge but an experiential revelation of who God is. The knowledge of His glory is released as we encounter Him and live based on the reality that He lives in us. We are carriers of His presence. As He manifests Himself to us, we learn who He is, allowing us to represent Him. As we live our daily life, we have an opportunity to offer people an encounter with the knowledge and revelation of who He is and what He is like. He lives in you and has clothed Himself with you in all of your uniqueness and beauty. Your life will impact the world around you, and together we will fill the earth with the revelation of who He is.

You are a carrier of the glory that fills the earth:

I have given them the *glory* that you gave me, that they may be *one* as we are *one.*

(John 17:22, NIV)

For God, who said "Let light shine out of darkness," made his light shine in our hearts to give us the light of the *knowledge of God's glory* displayed in the face of Christ.

(2 Cor. 4:6, NIV)

And we **all**, who with unveiled faces contemplate the Lord's glory, are being transformed into his image with ever-increasing glory, which comes from the Lord, who is the Spirit.

(2 Cor. 3:18, NIV)

We are *all* given this great invitation to encounter Him. This invitation is not only for ministers and preachers but also for all believers in Christ. The old covenant and law veils people's hearts from encountering Him for who He truly is. When Jesus came, the veil was removed. We, with an unveiled face, are able to speak plainly to God and behold Him for who He truly is.

As we behold who He is, we encounter His face—the image of who He truly is, His character, His nature, and His likeness. As we contemplate Him—look at and behold Him with continual attention—we are being transformed into His image with ever-increasing glory. As we behold His glorious face, shining like the sun (Rev. 1:16), shining upon us (Num. 6:24), we also shine with radiance and glory.

Transfigured

I realized that when I behold Him for who He really is, He also reveals who I really am. Seeing myself the way He sees me transforms me into the very image He has dreamed me to be from the beginning of time. As we continually look at and behold ourselves for who we truly are, we will be transformed and transfigured into our true identity. As God continually empowers us and encourages us from glory to glory, we shine bright with the radiance of the glory He reveals in us.

Let His words and His truth define you. Think upon it over and over. Write down what you hear God speaking over your life. Read it again out loud over yourself. Record it on an MP3 player. My husband and I write everything down and read it again over ourselves and over each other. We also let recordings play before we go to sleep. You can even soak in His word as you sleep. It is vital that you are transformed into the image of His truth and who He says you are, rather than being influenced by what the world has taught you, how you've been raised, or your past before you came to know Jesus.

> And have put on the new self who is being renewed to a true knowledge according to the image of the One who created him.
>
> (Col. 3:10, NASB)

As we remember who He says we truly are, we are being renewed to the "true knowledge" of the image of the One who created us. So when you look into your bathroom mirror, see yourself for who you really are. Do not allow a single thought in your mind to tell you who you are not. Agree with His truth in your life. Replay what He says about you over and over like it is the first time you have heard it. In doing this, you put on your new self—displaying beauty and glory.

The Greatest Movement
This is the greatest movement, and you are part of it. This is a movement of His sons and daughters arising, shining, and filling the earth with the knowledge and revelation of who God is. This is more than a revival in one place. This is a movement of His glory on us and in us as His whole body manifests God's power and glory over all the earth. We will cover the earth as the waters cover the sea, and you are part of it. This movement is here now, and it is ever increasing.

This book is an invitation for you to know God and know yourself even more. As a son or daughter, you are one with the Father, Son, and the Holy Spirit. Jesus lives and abides in you. Often in church services, we call out to God, asking Him to come to us, come meet us. However, how can you get any closer to someone that lives in you? How strange would it be if you were married and your spouse was in the same room with you, sitting right next to you, and you were still calling out for him or her to come? How strange would it be if you only talked to your spouse on a particular day of the week, ignoring each other every other moment despite your close proximity? And how would your relationship be if you only decided to sing songs to communicate instead of speaking plainly?

Being a son or daughter, you can talk to God openly in your own voice, using your own vocabulary and communication style. He is with you everywhere you go. This journey of relationship we are on is more about becoming aware of Him, rather than calling out to Him. Whether we feel Him or not, we live not from our feelings but from the reality of Him living inside of us. We can immediately start talking to Him plainly because He is already with us.

If we, in our thoughts and thinking, start thinking to God instead of thinking to ourselves, then we would invite Him into the conversation that we process in our minds, ultimately inviting Him into every situation and part of our lives. Why not? He is already there, living inside of you. By doing this we are acknowledging His presence and inviting Him to join the conversation. In this way, we position ourselves to hear His solutions, wisdom, and revelation over our situations and lives.

When you step outside or step into a room, you change the spiritual atmosphere around you to what you carry. You, wrapped up in His presence, are the answer the world has been longing for. You are a treasure chest, full of heaven, full of all He has invested in you! Wisdom and revelation are released wherever you go. He is with you and shares His secrets and solutions with you. You don't have to have it all figured out by yourself. You are His friend, and it is His great pleasure to give you the kingdom, all for the beauty and glory of how He is being revealed by your life. You are His dream! Everything you truly are will be released and the world around you will never be the same.

Dream His Dream
In this movement every person is created to be great and to live to their full potential. You are called to be great and nothing less. I

am confident of your greatness because the One who lives in you is not small but great!

This is His dream: that everyone steps into greatness, leaving no one behind. What would it look like if you and everyone around you were living to their full potential, living out their purposes and passions? Imagine that for a moment. Close your eyes and let the images play out. Take some time out to speak with God about His vision for the world and for you. Jesus, open our eyes to see Your dream!

What would it look like if everyone was living to their full potential? Take a moment to describe what that looks like.

As you are dreaming about this, here are a few questions to help prompt you:

Is everyone doing the same thing?

Is everyone working inside the church or on the mission field?

Are people having influence in business? In media? In other realms of life?

Do you see everyone around you as great?

Did you catch His vision? It is God's desire and passion that we all experience the fullness of life. Why else would He give us visions and dreams of beauty and success? He has such a beautiful heart and passion for seeing His beloved sons and daughters arising and shining.

Close your eyes and see it play out; do you see His sons and daughters arising and shining and covering the earth? God's desire is that everyone experiences the truth that they are needed and valuable, understanding his or her role in making the earth look like heaven.

Do you see it? Each person is meant to be a carrier of His glory, revelation, solutions, and wisdom. We are meant to be fully equipped for what every realm of influence needs. No limitations! As we arise and shine, it causes a domino effect—influencing other people to shine and arise to the greatness inside of them—until we cover the earth as the waters cover the sea.

See Yourself as Great
As you processed with God and dreamed about others stepping out in greatness, did you also see yourself as great? You are part of this great movement. Who you are—your unique piece of the picture—matters. We need all hands on deck if we are going to have an impact in every realm of influence and cover the world with His glory and goodness.

It is extremely important that you see yourself as great and that you understand the significance of your role in life. You are called to be great! Sometimes we can see other people as being great, but we can forget that our role and our place in the world are also of value and significance. You are part of the beautiful picture of what this world could become. You are completely necessary to the plans God has for the earth.

Take a little more time to ask God what His dream is for you. Write down what you hear Him say.

While you answered the questions above, as you began to see everyone around you as great, where were you in the picture?

What are you doing?

Who are you influencing?

Father, I ask in this moment that You would show them as they close their eyes what You dreamed about them before they were born. What does their greatness look like?

I am convinced each and every person needs to feel significant. We need to be recognized. We need to be encouraged and loved. We need relationship and family. We are created for this. Give yourself permission to experience these things and to see yourself as great.

See yourself arising from the place where circumstances have kept you. Arise and take action! Arise to new life! Shine! Be radiant! The Lord has risen upon you, and His glory will be seen in you. Every person you come into contact with will come to see God and experience His presence. It is attractive and contagious.

Being a Catalyst
One day the Father showed me a vision that played out in my mind like a movie. We were all on the frontline of battle. It was a war scene like William Wallace or David and Goliath, except each person fighting in this battle was on the front lines of their realm of influence. I was encouraging each individual, "You are bold, courageous! What you carry is important! You are unique! You are needed! You are necessary! What you are doing is not little; it is great!"

In the vision, I was speaking these truths over each person, eliminating any fear that could enter their souls. By calling out who they truly are, it meant that depression, despair, anxiety, hopelessness, and fear had to go. I continued to declare over them,

"You are loved! You are His Beloved! You were created to love and be loved! Now go take over the world in your realm of influence. You are ready. You were born for this!" I said these things with such confidence in them. My face radiated and shone with joy and delight like our heavenly Father.

What a joy it is to live from a perspective of encouragement and love for people. I am an encourager and a dreamer who dreams over people and their lives. I am a catalyst, cheering people on, investing in them, giving them hope and a reason to not give up. I am called to empower others and set them up for success. My purpose is to give His sons and daughters a safe place to encounter their heavenly Father—a place where they hear His voice, find their home, resting place, encouragement, and joyful bliss in His heart. As people learn to recognize IIis voice for themselves and others, it becomes a normal part of their lives, like breathing—continual, constant, and nonstop.

As you read this, I pray that the catalyst inside of you is awakened. That your unique ability to inspire and empower others increases, as does your ability to receive ideas and solutions that bring the optimal change and impact in your realm of influence.

The Importance of Vision

Where there is no vision, the people perish.

(Prov. 29:18, KJV)

I interpret this verse in two ways, both important in our understanding of who we are and what we are meant to accomplish in life. If you have no vision for your life, the passion inside of you is perishing. Life becomes a pattern: get up, eat breakfast, go to work, come home, sleep, and repeat. Every day becomes mundane. Where you lack vision, you are robbing your life of its full potential. Your passions are a great indicator of what your vision in life is. Grab hold of your passions and dream with God. Your passions are the fuel for your life. With vision, you are an unstoppable force, continually burning for a greater purpose. Just as you learned to recognize your value and greatness, give yourself permission to dream and dream big with no limits. The world is waiting for you.

The second interpretation of the verse is that if your vision doesn't happen, if it doesn't come to pass, then the people perish. Like Joseph and many other leaders in the Bible, if their vision or purpose on the earth hadn't come to pass, then the people would have perished. If your vision and God's dream for your life don't come to pass, the people you were called to impact will not be impacted. That sounds extreme, but it is true. Think about that for a moment. If you decide to quit pursuing your passions for any reason, the lives you were supposed to impact will not be impacted. Maybe God will bring another person around to do it—He is so good like that—however, the people around you won't be impacted the way you were meant to impact them.

I once had a strong desire to quit what I was doing. My husband and I were leading an incredible group of people. However, I was disconnected in some relationships within the group. Relationships are what make my life rich and enjoyable; they are like heaven on earth to me. When I have close-knit relationships—full of life, love, and joy—ministry does not feel like work. Things are smooth and light when we are operating with connection.

Experiencing these disconnects was painful, and it felt so much harder to do what we were doing. It seemed like I was going full force when some people who mattered the most to me appeared to be pulling back. I thought, *Someone else can do what I am doing; this is getting too difficult.*

However, as I started to invite in the idea of quitting, I immediately felt a groaning come from my spirit. The Holy Spirit showed me the people and families that I would influence. The Holy Spirit groaned within me for these people. He longed for them, and He longed for me to partner with Him to bring change in their lives.

This experience of feeling God's heart for these people strengthened me and shifted my focus. It suddenly became all about impacting these lives. Don't let quitting be a solution to your problem or relief from the pain you feel. Let God come with promises over the situations you are facing. Ask Him what to believe about the situation and who He will be for you in the situation. If you quit, the people around you will not be impacted. If you choose to pursue vision and purpose, the lives you were called to impact will be forever changed.

Activation Journeys

My husband, Huub, and I have a passion to see people's lives changed in God's presence, as the lies people once believed are demolished by God's love and truth. We thrive giving prophetic, encouraging words and loving on His beautiful sons and daughters, activating and awakening others to be more aware of His presence and the host of heaven.

Through each chapter I want to invite you to experience God's presence and His love for you. As we journey through this book, there will be times when you are prompted to dream with your heavenly Father. I will ask you questions throughout each chapter, and I encourage you to write down your responses. This is an interactive book, an invitation to process what you are discovering and come to your own conclusions and revelations.

Don't be discouraged if you feel like you have a hard time hearing from God. When you are prompted to listen for God's voice, write down the first thing that comes to your mind. What do you sense, feel, hear, or see? Write it down or maybe even draw it out. After you've written or drawn it, then you can examine it and see if it was from Him.

Your best gauge for determining if you are hearing God's voice is to ask yourself if what you've received makes you feel empowered, encouraged, comforted, loved and if it pulls you closer to the Father. In my own experience, even when God corrects me, I am still empowered and full of hope to overcome. The enemy is the one who lies, condemns, separates, and steals hope, disempowering us. He comes to steal, kill, and destroy.

Huub and I were doing a prophetic school, and we told everyone to write a love letter from the Father. Afterward, we asked if everyone would share what they wrote down. One of the students said, "I'm not sharing. There is no way it came from God! It came too easy. It is also way too good to be true." We respected their decision not to share and went on to the next person. I had already written down an encouraging word for the student who refused to share, and so after everyone was finished, I shared the word with that student, who was deeply moved and said, "What you shared is what I wrote down." I told the student, "You do hear His voice! And it is easier than you think." He is the shepherd and His sheep hear His voice. He is such a good and loving Father, and it is easier to hear Him than we realize.

I encourage you to enjoy each journey we go on together with the Father. Write down everything He is saying to you and revealing to you. This book may be a quick read, but I encourage you to let things affect you on a deeper level so that by the end of this book, you will have life-giving encounters and be forever changed.

You are a very valuable, needed part of this great movement. You may have some questions as we get started. How does this practically play out? Is there some practical application and activation? What is true greatness and success? What is the greatness I carry? What is it that I am called to? How do I get encouraged when it seems like no one is encouraging me? These are excellent questions. Let me take you on a journey together with your heavenly Father to discover the answers.

CHAPTER 2
BE REVEALED

What is the greatness you carry? It is often much easier to see what gifts and talents other people have and what their passions are, because you operate differently than they do. Who they are is easy to recognize. You are affected and influenced by the uniqueness of who they are. You notice them because they are different from who you are and what you do and what you are passionate about. And through your eyes they are AMAZING!

However, recognizing and discovering what you carry—the gifts, passions, talents, and what you are called to—can be difficult because it is normal to you. You were created for a purpose, and the things you love and excel at shouldn't be hard for you. It shouldn't be work for you to be you.

If I were you for a day, I would get to see the world through your eyes. I would experience what you're passionate about—what consumes your thoughts all day long and the things that are truly important to you. I would see what grieves you, what you will fight for, and what truly makes you come alive. I would clearly understand what changes you want to see in the world around you.

What if I am able to highlight those things to you and help you see how unique and necessary you are? I would be able to tell you how great your passions are, the impact you are having on the world around you, and the legacy you are sure to leave. Your ideas and dreams are truly a gift. If you recognized the beauty you carry, you would view yourself differently. You would see yourself the way He sees you. You would see your value and significance.

I love to partner with the Father and let Him highlight people's unique characteristics and the beauty they carry. This is something we can all do. Start by asking Him questions about others, and let Him reveal the people around you. As you begin to see their unique qualities, encourage them with what you see and hear. And, of course, we can use the same practice in our own lives by asking the Father what unique gifts, talents, and passions He placed inside of you.

He dreamed about you from the beginning of time. He created and invested in you; all you have to do is ask Him to empower you to see each investment He made in you as beautiful, powerful, and unique. Ask God how you can influence and bring solutions to the world around you in the areas you are passionate about. Become aware of the glory you carry inside of you, and release it to the world. Be you and the fullness of the beauty of who you are.

Be True and Authentic to Who You Are
In 1 Samuel 17, David took on Goliath. David was true to himself and his personal journey with God. When Saul gave him his armor to wear, he didn't wear it because he wasn't used to it. He did not care that the armor was the king's or that it was shiny and extravagant. His way was unique—how David operated with the Father didn't look successful to anyone else, but he remained true to himself. He couldn't use Saul's armor, David had His own journey with

God and knew what worked for him. All he needed was a stone, a slingshot, and His God.

What is "Saul's armor" in your life? We could look at other people and other ministries and admire how successful they are. In our admiration of others, we could think their way is the exact way we should follow or think their message is more powerful or successful, not realizing the significance of our own.

Don't be an echo of what other people are saying and doing. Even though it may seem great, take from others what fits you and continue on your own journey of life with the Father. You don't have to wear Saul's armor or kill Goliath with a slingshot. Go on your own journey and adventures with God, ask Him questions regarding your situation, and receive solutions. Pursue His heart, and together the impossible can happen!

Be genuine and authentic to who you are. Stay close to yourself, and live out your original expression. Discover it and see it as important and of great value. Whenever I encourage someone to sing, write a book, or do anything in life, I encourage them not to be a duplicate but rather a unique sound the world has never heard before. No one's DNA strand is like yours, no one has your voice or your perspective, and no one else ever will. In the church we often talk about a new sound—looking for and longing for this new thing. What is the new sound? I am convinced the new sound is you! You have the opportunity to be a sound no one has heard before. You have this one life to be the most authentic sound, message, and expression the world has ever encountered before or after you.

While at a leaders' conference, the guest speaker shared about having an impact on our cities. He said that if a church is apostolic, then our measuring stick of being apostolic would be how our city is impacted. I wholeheartedly support this message and the speaker. However, I was concerned that the leaders would think this means they should model what has worked for the person speaking.

Leaving the meeting, the sound of people's chatter filled my ears and the room. Some leaders came up to me afterward and said, "We've always had a heart for our city. However, how do we impact it?" What a beautiful heart they have, and my response and encouragement to them and everyone is to stay true to themselves. If you want to have an impact, then love on your city and serve it with the gifts and talents that you have and with the passion that bubbles up naturally inside of you. Live from this place of who you are, and it won't feel like work. Become aware of the gifts and the talents you carry, and use them to bless the people around you. We can have the greatest impact by realizing what is inside of us and using that to bless and serve the people around us.

Called Outside the Church

It is just as spiritual to be called outside of the church as it is to be called to serve in the church. Daniel and Joseph excelled at everything they did. They were great leaders and had a historical impact. They were not called to the church or synagogue. They had a historical impact outside of the church with their dream interpretation, wisdom, revelation, and prophetic insight. They served rulers who were evil, much more evil than we would consider a lot of our bosses. Daniel and Joseph were heavenly expressions and displays of the power of God in their workplace. Joseph was a prisoner who made the prison better with his wisdom, revelation, knowledge, and excellence. His actions pointed straight to the God he served.

There are numerous heroes in the Bible who were not called to the church. Instead, these individuals were called to have an impact on people, cities, and nations outside the church. We need to catch this revelation that it is not more spiritual to be involved in the church. If that were the case, what would that say to those who are truly not called to the church?

My husband, Huub, works as Senior Team Lead in CRM. And when he goes into work, the impact he has there is no less spiritual than when he and I lead prophetic schools and speak or usher people into God's manifested presence. We all need to be fully empowered in our places of influence, wherever that may be. Every person needs to be fully equipped for the works of ministry. Every CEO, singer, songwriter, politician, manager, teacher, and professor should be fully equipped and operating in the fullness of wisdom, revelation, healing, and prophetic insight. What would the world look like if we were fully equipped, empowered, believed in, and encouraged? What would our schools look like? What would companies look like? Perhaps it would look like the glory of the revelation of God covering the earth.

Be Who You Are Everywhere You Go
My husband, Huub, is always authentically himself everywhere he goes. He loves the people in front of him whether he is at church, the supermarket, or the office. He hears the Father's thoughts for people and shares it with them. He supports his colleagues and does what he can to set them up for success. At his work, when things are extremely difficult and people don't know what to do, he has become known as a stable place that is secure and brings peace in the midst of chaos.

Often Huub is assigned the hardest projects. Some people wouldn't dare to do some of the projects that Huub jumps into, yet those hard projects become a success. Why? Because the Father encourages him through it all saying, "Huub, I am with you. You are my beloved son.

Yes, go for it! I will make this project a success!" So Huub closes his eyes to the impossible and jumps into projects, listening to the Father continually believe in him and give him the solutions he needs.

There are times when he experiences opposition—colleagues not supporting him during a meeting or on projects. In those moments, Huub hears the Father cheering him on and encouraging him. Sometimes Huub has no idea how to fix a problem on a specific project. On several occasions he had a dream at night and from the dream was able to draw out the solution the next day for his colleagues. We are in awe of God and all the ways he chooses to speak to us and partner with us. It is true that with God nothing is impossible. These experiences aren't just for Huub—God is with you and supports you. He prospers everything you put your hands to. This is why it is so important that we shine and bring His glory—the glory we carry inside—into our places of influence.

Ask Jesus right now what gift, talent, or wisdom is unique to you. What is it that you carry that you can impart to others? Why is this characteristic so important? How can you impact the world around you—family, friends, and coworkers—with what is inside of you? How can you bless them and love them? Ask God to fill you with love for them. What does He like about them? What is His dream over them, and how can you make that dream come true? Now watch as you and the Father become a beautifully orchestrated love explosion impacting the lives around you. No one can have the exact impact you have; believe in yourself and be confident in it. You will radiate and shine with the authenticity of who you are. Your life is the most powerful message for the world to hear.

A Visual Display of His Glory

I've heard people boldly speaking the scripture, "God raised us up with Christ and seated us with him in the heavenly realms"

(Eph. 2:6, NIV). I've heard people declaring it, shouting it out. The reality is we *are* seated with Him in the heavenly realms. It is vital that we become aware of where we are seated and learn to operate in our daily life from that place. Through this verse, the Father is revealing something about Himself—His plans for us and the world.

> But **because of his great love for us**, God, **who is rich in mercy**, made us **alive** with Christ even when we were dead in transgressions—it is by grace you have been saved. And God raised us up with Christ and seated us with him in the heavenly realms in Christ Jesus.

> (Eph. 2:4–6, NIV)

"Because of His great love for us"—He is so rich in mercy that He made us alive to a new position on the earth. In Christendom, so much focus is placed on being dead with Christ. We were dead in our transgressions, but now we are alive. You are no longer dead. You are only dead to sin. It no longer has a hold on you. You are alive, and there is a great reason why He caused you to live. His resurrection power looks like something. Being a Christian was never meant to be boring but exciting, glorious, and powerful. Being alive and expressing the fullness of who you are brings Him glory!

You are His son or daughter who was meant to live in the reality of heaven on the earth. He didn't leave you where you were dead in your old life. He took you out of that place and brought you into His house, His supernatural realm, which is the natural realm for Him. It should be natural for you as well. You have access to Jesus and everything available in heaven. Whether you are aware of it or not, you are seated in heavenly realms and have the ability to impact the earth with what is available in heaven.

It is vital that you come to the awareness of where you are seated. How unfortunate for you and the world around you to be closed off to what has been made available to you. Become aware of what is available to you everywhere you go. What does it look like to be seated in heavenly realms next to Jesus? How close is heaven? How easy is it to access? When Jesus prayed, "On earth as it is in heaven" (Matt. 6:10), it was from a place of understanding that you and I are portals, carriers, and releasers of heaven wherever we go. In this we see God revealing Himself as a loving, mighty, merciful Father who desires us to come fully alive. He is restoring us to our place of connection and oneness, where we are seated with Him. He is so much better than we think.

Why have you been seated with Christ in the heavenly places?

> In order that in the coming ages he might show the incomparable riches of his grace, expressed in his kindness to us in Christ Jesus. For it is by grace you have been saved, through faith—and this is not from yourselves, it is the gift of God—not by works, so that no one can boast.

> (Eph. 2:7–9, NIV)

You are seated in the heavenly realms so that He might display the immeasurable, incomparable riches of His grace and kindness through you! What does that look like? Your life is a beautiful display rich in His grace and loving kindness. Every Christian, at some point, knows what it is to live a life without Jesus. We all at some point asked Him into our lives, and our lives should display His restoration. Who I am today, everything in my life that is beautiful is because of His love and restoration. He has restored my family. If I were to tell you stories today of where I came from, you wouldn't believe me. My life is a visual display of His goodness. My life is a glistening beacon of hope for others to walk in.

In every area of my life, He has restored me back into His heart and freedom.

I know what it means to be lost, searching my whole life for love and not finding it. When God revealed Himself to me, I realized I finally found the One I had been looking for. No one needed to tell me to spend time with God. I was so excited to see what He would do next! I would run into my room, shut the door, and lavish my love on Him and ask Him questions. He showed me visions—promises of where I would go. He showed me what He was going to do in my life—His plans and purposes. I had never seen visions like that before. I was captivated as I wrote everything down or drew pictures of what I saw.

Everywhere I went, He would speak to me, and I would test it out. I was learning to recognize His voice. He showed me visions and promises over other people's lives. I would write them down or draw it out and give it away. I was in awe that what He was revealing to me was true and came to pass. This empowered me even more. I thought if I spent my whole day in His presence receiving wisdom and revelation and experiencing who He is, I could change the world. This is the place we are seated and get to live from. And together, you and I, we will change the world in the riches of His grace, loving kindness, and knowledge of the glory of the Lord revealing who He is! All these things we experience reveal who He is and wants to be for the world and for us.

Have you ever been devastated by what you see going on in the world around you? The same mercy and goodness He has displayed for you is also available for every person. It is our job and honor to display what a restored relationship with Him looks like. Sometimes, I would rather not share my past because of the devastation and shame I experienced. I would rather forget about it and not remember it, live as though it never happened. However, when I open my heart and am vulnerable, I am a visual display of His redemptive work. There was nothing I could do to earn it—He freely lavishes His love on me. It is an entirely humbling experience and revelation. And at the same time, my heart is bursting with thankfulness. I am who I am today because of His great love and mercy. I will embrace those broken pieces to reveal His goodness and loving kindness in my life because as I share His glory and goodness it calls others home to His heart.

He has made you come alive—restored your life. How can we hold all this goodness in and enjoy it for only ourselves? Let thankfulness for who He is be your passion and fuel to display His beauty even more. You are a glorious beacon of His goodness—a living visual display and expression of who the Father is and has been in your life.

Right now, wherever you are as you read this book, you are also seated in heavenly places. You are a traveling heavenly portal. It is important that you continually become aware and operate from this place and position. You are meant to operate from this beautiful connection with the Father displaying His glorious wonders for yourself and others around you. Wherever you go, you're a portal, a gateway of heaven being released on earth.

Be Revealed

> For the creation waits in eager expectation for the children of God to be revealed.

> (Rom. 8:19, NIV)

The whole earth is waiting and groaning for you to discover who you are and the glory that will be revealed in you. You are His beloved son, His beloved daughter, living in a beautiful, constant two-way friendship and relationship. What will your life and the fullness of your beauty look like displayed on the earth? The whole of creation is waiting for you to discover who you are, what you carry as a son and a daughter. The world is waiting in eager expectation for who you are to be displayed on the earth and to be revealed.

Before you can be revealed, you must first realize who you are and what you carry. Let God reveal who you are. Ask Him questions about who you are—it is truly that simple. Receiving your significance from Him causes you to be confidant that your role, your unique talents, gifts, and purpose are important and necessary. As I said before, this is tricky because what you do, your passions in life, are normal to you. However, this step is important in discovering yourself because the world is waiting to see your unique, authentic beauty.

> Because the creation itself also shall be delivered from the bondage of corruption into the glorious liberty of the children of God.
>
> (Rom. 8:21, NKJV)

God's creation, people who don't know Him, are in the bondage of corruption, enslaved in sin, groaning for their deliverance. Like orphans on the search for their biological parents, so are His sons and daughters searching to know where they came from and who their true Father is. They don't know how to get free but are eagerly expecting to discover the truth. As you are revealed, so is God. You represent who He is and what He is like. As a visual display of His glory and goodness you become a revelation of hope, revealing what they have been searching for their whole life. You become an invitation into the same glorious liberty you've been given as you display what that looks like to be free, liberated, restored, and brought into new life and true identity.

So don't hide. Let go of anything that holds you back. You are light to the world. Let who you are and who the Father has been for you be expressed from every part of you. As you step into a room, everything comes into submission to the King and His kingdom. As you occupy and represent who He is and His kingdom in your place of business, church, and family, He will speak with you as a friend and will give you wisdom and revelation for that place. It is His desire to give us the kingdom, and you are here to ensure that His kingdom comes, and that the world receives the things He has made available for each person.

Be confident like a city on a hill that cannot be hidden (Matt. 5:14). Your light—who you are—dispels darkness. Break agreement with any lie that would hold you back from this truth. The earth is waiting and groaning for you to be revealed. The ones who don't know who their Father is are waiting for you to be revealed. They are waiting for your piece, your unique expression to be revealed on the earth so that they will know who He is and come home into His heart.

Be Fueled by Your Passion

I love to ask people what they are passionate about, activating them to pursue it in the present and not to let it remain an idea for the distant future. What do you want to see changed now? What are you passionate about in what you do? Why do you do what you do? I sit on the edge of my seat waiting to hear what they will share because as they do, visions and dreams dance in my head. Dreams of how they will have a great impact and ideas and steps of how they can do it.

I have a friend who is an elementary teacher. She is so beautiful and pure-hearted. One day we were talking, and I asked her what she was passionate about. She said she has a passion for instilling identity in the children she teaches. That is her goal every day for the time that she gets to spend with the kids each year before they move on. I could see the emotions on her face as she shared her passion. She gives one hundred percent of herself for this purpose. She said, "Sometimes I go home, and I am hard on myself thinking, *What could I have done to do more?*" She has such a beautiful passion for impacting these children's lives.

I asked her what it would look like if she could instill identity in even more children, reaching further than her classroom. As she thought about that, I asked, "Have you ever thought about writing a children's book? Or maybe some music with your husband?" She was surprised, "Write books? I could never do that!" she said. I assured her that she can do anything. We live in the information age. If she wanted to write a book there is enough information about how to do it. It is so much easier than we think. If we believe in our message, it will be the passion that drives us through any obstacle.

Sometimes we should dream much bigger and ask ourselves about these passions that live within us. If you believe in your passion and take time to dream over it, you could have an even greater impact. In my friend I see this beautiful treasure, and I don't want it to be hidden. Everyone she touches should be rich with the treasure she has. What are those things in your life? What are those treasures and passions you reveal without even knowing it? What thoughts spin in your mind each day at work or when you go home? Think about it for a moment. Ask the Father to highlight them to you. They may seem normal to you, so take time to recognize what God is saying. Ask Jesus, "Will you come and bring to remembrance the passions I have to make a change? To see an impact?" Write the thoughts that first come to mind. Now dream with the Lord about how you can have greater impact or what you need in order to live based on that passion.

What training do you need in order to accomplish what God just revealed to you? Go for it! Don't sit back and tell yourself it is impossible. There is so much knowledge and information available at our fingertips. Make time for it, practice, and excel. Don't let the lie come in telling you that you don't have that gift of writing, teaching, singing, playing music, or healing the sick. In every realm of influence, you will need training. Be teachable and expandable. Ask God for favor and opportunities, for doors to open up where you can get trained. This applies to spiritual and natural gifts. He said to prophesy, raise the dead, and heal the sick! Sounds like a great commission to me. Sometimes we need to practice and try things out in a safe environment. Go to a healing school or a prophetic training school even if you don't think of yourself as prophetic. It is for you. Learn to recognize His voice for yourself and others.

Operating in the prophetic realm and encouraging people fits every area of influence. Receiving insight and solutions for people, tasks, and assignments and encouraging people with His thoughts for them should be part of our everyday lives. You could be prophesying or encouraging people without them knowing it. When they ask how you knew this, you can reveal the Father who saw them and gave you the revelation. Don't let anything stop you. Find people around you who will celebrate you and the risks you take.

After you get some training, step out and practice it continually so you can experience how you operate with the Father, just like David did. Be yourself. The most important part of training is practicing because in practicing we learn. Even if you don't get it right the first time, you are learning and growing. Look back after you've practiced, and see how far you've come. As you practice your passion, give people an encounter with love and encouragement. Love never fails. Believe in your message and let that passion inside of you be your driving force to overcome any obstacle and reveal God's love to the world.

Activation: Dreaming with the Father
Take a moment and dream—with no limitations and no excuses. Give yourself permission to dream. And when you receive insight, write it down or type it up.

1. Ask the Holy Spirit the following questions:

   Highlight the things in my life that seem natural for me but are truly unique gifts from You.

   What do I carry that You see as important and great?

   Jesus, what do You see in me?

   Jesus, what do You like about me?

2. Ask yourself some questions:

   What am I passionate about?

   What would I love to see change the most in the world around me?

   What things in my area of influence would I love to see change the most?

What does it look like for me to be seated in heavenly places? What does that mean for me? What has been available to me in Heaven, the fruits and gifts of the spirit? Being a portal and carrier of heaven, how can I release these things in the world around me?

3. As you discover your passions, ask the Father how you can influence the world around you with those passions. List them out, and dream with Him about it. Let your mind wander and see problems and ask for solutions.

4. Find friends and people in your life who, when you are around them, make you come alive—ones who inspire you when you dream together. Find people who can ask you some good questions and who can dream with you. Try out new ideas and dream big, with no limits. Begin to recognize and see that what's inside of you is a gift and that it is important. He set you on this earth for a reason. You are unique, and what you carry is of great value to the world around you.

CHAPTER 3

DEFINING SUCCESS

I went on a journey years ago to find out what true success and greatness looks like to me. It is important to discover what success means to you so that no one else can define it for you. Success is different for everyone. We must first redefine what we have been taught in this world—whether identifying the measuring stick by which we feel measured or understanding how we choose to measure others.

What is true success and greatness? Some find it in numbers. Some find it in titles or in ministry. Some may think to be great is to remain the greatest. We live in a competitive market where we want all the people to come to us, to use our services. We want to be their first choice. A singer wants to be number one on the charts, always. There is no problem with being number one or being great in your business, gifting, or talent. Arise and shine! Be amazing! Win! However, we bypass significance and purpose when we wrap our identity in our titles and in what we do, losing sight of the purpose for doing the things we do.

In my own life, I know success needs to be redefined when situations arise that cause insecurities to pop up unusually or when I have a need to feel significant or to be recognized. In those moments, I always take a step back and refocus. I ask myself important questions: *What is the result I want to leave behind in this situation? Why do I do what I do?* I visualize it and determine whether or not the visualized outcome is really my goal. If so, I go for it! In every situation, I focus on discovering what success is for me. I grab hold of that with everything and let that determine my choices and my responses. I have discovered that success is so much easier than we have made it out to be. It is so liberating and freeing to know your own definition of success and not live based on the definition of others. I hope that as you read this book, it will take you on a journey of discovering what true success is for your life. When discovering it for yourself, no one else can define it for you.

The Baptism Competition

> After this, Jesus and his disciples went out into the Judean countryside, where he spent some time with them and baptized. Now John also was baptizing at Aenon near Salim, because there was plenty of water, and people were coming and being baptized. (This was before John was put in prison.) An argument developed between some of John's disciples and a certain Jew over the matter of ceremonial washing. They came to John and said to him, "Rabbi, that man who was with you on the other side of the Jordan—the one you testified about—look, he is baptizing, and everyone is going to him."

> (John 3:22–26, NIV)

John the Baptist was known as the greatest. We refer to him as John-the-Baptist; it is both his name and his title. We don't know him simply as John; in fact, no one even calls him by his real last name. We know him as John the Baptist. I wonder how many people actually even know his last name. Jesus himself said that no one born of a woman has been greater than John the Baptist (Matt. 11:11). Let's catch a glimpse of what Jesus defines as great:

> To this John replied, "A person can receive only what is given them from heaven. You yourselves can testify that I said, 'I am not the Messiah but am sent ahead of him.' The bride belongs to the bridegroom. The friend who attends the bridegroom waits and listens for him, and is full of joy when he hears the bridegroom's voice. That joy is mine, and it is now complete. He must become greater; I must become less."
>
> (John 3:27–30, NIV)

I love what John the Baptist answered to those who wanted to compete and define his success. He said that a man receives nothing—no office or function in life—unless it has been given to him from heaven. He explained what his function was. He was very confident in who he was, his role in life, and what he would do. He saw it as a gift that was given to him by the Father.

I have clung to this revelation and truth in my life in so many situations. I have become confident in this truth that John the Baptist revealed in his answer. If he hadn't realized that his role in life was a gift and was important, if he didn't have a revelation of what success was for himself, he could have let other people define it for him. He wouldn't have been confident in his role and purpose. He could have listened to them and worked hard at recruiting more people to come and get baptized. Maybe that would have worked out for him for a while. I can imagine that it would have been very exhausting.

If John hadn't held to the truth of his role, he would have lost focus of what he was supposed to be doing, making the task at hand more difficult than necessary. He would have lost sight of his purpose on the earth, calling people to himself and going against the very thing he was meant to do.

Instead, John was confident, content, and even full of joy in his role. He didn't compare himself to others. He embraced the gift and role he had in life. He didn't let others define what success or greatness meant in his own life. He didn't need to keep his status, and he certainly didn't need to continue being the greatest of all baptizers. His life was based on the passion and joy of what his role in life was: to prepare the way of the Lord and to point everyone to Jesus. He let that be his focus, and he chose not to be distracted from it.

Success Is Revealing the Father

In John 3:30, John the Baptist said that Jesus must become greater, and he [John] must become less. Some translations quote him as saying, "I must decrease that He may increase." I don't believe John was saying "Oh, my flesh, my stinkin' flesh...Let there be none of me and all of you, God!" I believe he was saying that his title as the greatest needed to decrease so that the name of Jesus could increase and be known.

Imagine if we lived our lives with this same intention. As Christians, we are called to make the name of Jesus known far above our own names. When we receive recognition or acknowledgment for healing the sick, raising the dead, delivering and setting people free—all of those things must reveal who He is as we revel and glory in Him—His goodness and loving kindness. Let it be that our lives and greatness cause people to come into an encounter with our heavenly Father and His greatness. As we step out, people should become awed by Him and not who He is working through. We are to be a visual display of His goodness and glory, a walking, living expression of who He is because He has revealed Himself to us and we mirror that same image.

I believe God wants us to be all that we were created to be, to live in the fullness of who we are. I don't believe that we can't be well known. Unfortunately, we as Christians have shied away from the desire to win or to want to win because it seems prideful. But it isn't. Go for it! Dream great! Be great! Just don't let your identity get wrapped around how great you are, thinking that you have to hold that place or position at any cost. Your position doesn't define you. Like John the Baptist, focus on why you do what you do.

Become confident that everything you are and your role in life is great! You are a gift from the Father. Who you are is so important, needed, and necessary! Carry that in every situation. Be successful in fulfilling your unique purpose. Your heavenly Father dreamed about you before the beginning of time. Let the words the Father and Jesus spoke over you shape and mold you into His truth. I can imagine that John heard Jesus call him great, and that impacted him. Jesus loved John the Baptist. It is so important that you hear what Jesus, the Father, and the Holy Spirit say about you. Let His truth and His love define you. Be His dream come true on the earth.

Who Are We Revealing?
Let His name increase and our name decrease. What I mean by that is, when we tell people stories and testimonies, what will people leave our conversation with? Will they be wowed by how we share our encounters? Will they say, "Wow, she has dreamed all night long, has visions in detail with amazing colors, and can prophesy the most accurate words!" "He is being caught up into heaven." "They have angelic encounters!" "What amazing revelation they have!"

Who are we really revealing—the Father or ourselves? Having dreams, visions, prophetic words, healing, and revelation should be normal for Christians. You are His son or daughter—He reveals His secrets and mysteries to you. Greater encounters of who He is await us because we are shifting our focus to the One who is giving the revelation and the great reason why He gave it. Get ready to be in awe and fall deeper in love with who He is.

Everything should flow from our connection and relationship with Him; and that is the most beautiful thing of all. We are so rich in Him. The gifts of prophecy and healing, words of knowledge, and dreams and visions should flow from our relationship, love, and passion for Him and for the person we're ministering to. When we encounter Him and are overwhelmed with His love, we then become a beautiful, living expression of who He is.

If hearing His voice is difficult for you at this moment, become like a child and ask the Father to reveal Himself in a new way. When you wake up, and during your day, become aware of His delight for you. Ask Him what He thinks about you. Write it down. Ask Him questions. Be a great receiver of His love. Give yourself permission to be overwhelmed by Him, and let His love go deep. Meditate and bask in it. After receiving such great love, how could you not lavish your love on Him? It will pour out of you from a place of passion and connection.

I have experienced people reveal Him in ways I don't believe are expressions of the Father. As people reveal Him, I ask myself, *Is what they are sharing coming from a place of love and relationship?* People sometimes learn to operate out of their gifting—a formula they've been taught—and not out of relationship. Gifting doesn't equal having a close relationship with God.

Another question I often ask is whether or not the person is operating out of mercy or judgement. Mercy triumphs over judgement. Is mercy their heart posture? When you encounter Him, you should become like Him, mirroring and revealing His image. Jesus cried out, "Father, forgive them, for they do not know what they do" (Luke 23:34, NKJV). He disregarded any shame, rejection, and hate from people, and He walked with this joy continually set before him. What is His joy? It is His children. We are His joy! Even the ones who have not yet come home are His joy. Instead of prophesying doom, gloom, and disaster, mirroring Him looks like interceding for people who are in deep, deep darkness. Our prayer should be that they will arise, shine, and come into an encounter with His heart.

Playing to Win

Do you play to win? I am very competitive when it comes to games. I'm in it to win it! My husband and I enjoy playing the game Phase 10. I love asking the Holy Spirit what card to play; being like a child and practicing hearing the voice of the Holy Spirit has caused me to recognize His voice and leading. Sometimes I can be unsure, wondering if I really heard from the Holy Spirit or if I was only guessing.

However, one day my husband, Huub, and I were playing Phase 10 and a card in my hand was highlighted to me. My eyes were fixed on this specific card. I knew this was the card I needed to lay down! With extreme confidence, I laid the card on the table.

"Yes!" Huub exclaimed.

"What?" I shouted. I was sure I was supposed to play that card. What happened?

We continued to play. He laid down his card; then it was my turn again. As I listened for the direction of the Holy Spirit, I laid down the card confidently.

"YES!" Huub responded with great excitement. "This is EXACTLY, what I needed!"

I was in utter shock. I talked to the Holy Spirit, asking, "What is going on? I really felt like that was the card I was supposed to play. It looks like Huub is even about to win!" I did not like it one bit, let me tell you! I started telling the Holy Spirit how I was not enjoying the game. I love to win. "I know I am hearing your voice," I said to the Holy Spirit. "I know I am playing the right cards. However, I seem to be playing the very cards that Huub needs to win. What is going on?"

Then I heard the Father say to me, "Miranda, you'll know you're winning when others win." That immediately shifted my focus and deeply affected my heart. I sat there wrapping my mind around that, letting that definition of success sink in. By playing the cards I thought I was supposed to play, I was setting my husband up for success. I gave him everything he needed to win! He needed those cards I had in my hand, and I was to give them to him even if it didn't make me look very successful.

And then what? I thought. *Does that mean I lose?* No, He told me that I actually win when I give everything I can to set others up for success. That is my measuring stick for success. Seeing others grow, succeed, arise, and shine becomes my celebration. Those moments become my significance. I have wrestled with a lie that if I gave everything away, then I wouldn't be needed anymore. This very lie goes against what I was born for!

After the encounter I had while playing cards with Huub, I asked the Father to speak to me about the lie of not being needed anymore. The Lord shifted my focus off of me and on to the whole world. There will always be a need. The whole earth has not yet been filled with the revelation of the knowledge of His goodness and glory (Hab. 2:14). The world doesn't yet know that we are heavenly expressions living life on earth or that the earth is supposed to look like heaven. From that perspective, I can't give everything away quick enough!

I know I am winning or succeeding when I set others up for success. When they are thriving and winning, that is the measurement of my success. Let that be your new measure for success. Don't buy into the lie that as you give everything away you are somehow losing or appear to be less successful. You are succeeding. We need more people who will set others up for success. Who doesn't need a person like that in their life?

Support from the Heart
Part of helping others be successful is supporting them with your whole heart. Have you ever had someone new come into your company or church, and you were concerned about your position? What was happening in your heart when you had to work with them? Huub and I lead a prophetic school. One day someone new came into our church and decided that they were going to start a school that was pretty similar to what we were doing. They wanted to come to our school and meet the students, but I started to feel little insecurities pop up in my heart. Thoughts came into my mind that I tried to push down: *What if they take our students?* I loved what we were doing. I saw lives being changed, and now this new person wanted to come in and meet our students, but for what reason? In an effort to support this person, I pushed all of those thoughts aside and welcomed them with a smile on my face.

However, I knew what I was feeling inside was not good, and I knew I didn't want it.

I convinced myself to help this individual. As a longtime leader at the church, I had a lot of good ideas that could assist them. So I asked them, "Is there any way I can support you in what you are doing?"

"Nope, I've got it. Thanks!" that person replied.

For one split second, I thought to myself, *Yeah, let's see how that turns out.* Immediately I heard the Father say to me, "You can't afford for this person not to succeed!" All at once, His voice came with the revelation of knowing that everything Huub and I had given for this movement would need to be restored in each place this person didn't succeed. Hearts would need to be healed, and we would have even more work to do. His words melted my heart, and from that point on, I was able to support that person wholeheartedly.

This revelation changed my life forever. The Father showed me that He needs every person to succeed, and I am to do whatever I can to set them up for success. If they don't succeed, we have a bigger mess to clean up. He showed me that if I ever felt threatened by any ministry and let people proceed without my wholehearted support, we would not be as great as we could have been. I need everyone to succeed. I can't afford to let my heart disconnect from others.

Together, supporting each other, we will have the greatest impact. Join me in choosing to support people from your heart. Don't simply pray for people—pray outrageous prayers over them! Encourage them with what you hear the Father say about them. Ask Him what you are to believe about them. Receive His heart for them and declare His limitlessness over them so that they will be the best versions of themselves.

We are a team. The truth is, we need each other. You need the people around you to succeed. Set them up for success! Maybe you're not involved in what they are doing, but you can believe in them and encourage them. Don't shrink back from what others are doing. Life is so much richer this way.

Focus

Another important aspect of success is learning to focus. There are so many good things we can be doing in life. Some things are only meant for a season. How do you know what season you are in? Part of determining what you need to focus on is asking yourself some difficult questions. Are you able to let go of something you may have started, something for which you are well known and that is having a great impact? Are you able to let others step into your place? Is it time to step away from a task or duty for no other reason than because you know deep down inside that you're not supposed to do it anymore?

I was making myself lunch one day by boiling two eggs. The eggs I was using were one or two days over the expiration date. I put them in boiling water and set the timer. As they were cooking, I heard the Father speak to me and tell me to use the eggs that were new, and not expired. I thought, *Oh no, I don't want to waste the eggs I am preparing! They are still good to eat! What a waste if I throw them away.* Despite my internal struggle, I said to the Father, "Ok, I get it. You want to reveal something to me, just tell me so I don't have to waste those eggs." But He didn't speak any further. I waited and waited with the expectation that He was just going to tell me what was going on. But He didn't. I finally said, "Ok, ok! I will go along with it through the process." So I set aside the other pan with the old eggs in it, and took out a new pan and prepared the new eggs.

As those new eggs were cooking, I got a call from my mom. I missed my mom so much that I picked up the phone immediately, and we talked for a little while. As we were talking, the new eggs finished cooking, so I turned off the burner, and I set them by the other eggs. A few minutes later we hung up and I walk back into the kitchen to find out I didn't know which eggs were which! *Oh no!* I thought. *Which ones am I supposed to eat?* Then I heard Him say, "Touch the eggs, see which one is hotter" I put my hand on each egg, relieved to find it was easy to determine which the newer eggs were.

As I ate, the Father started revealing the meaning behind the eggs. There were a few things in my life that were expired. They were still good; there was nothing wrong with what I was doing. However, those things were expired. I needed to focus on some other things, particularly a new thing that was coming. It wasn't here yet; it was new and coming. The way I would know what things I was supposed to do was if they felt hot, if they were burning in my spirit.

I also knew that I was supposed to stop doing Sozo, an inner-healing ministry. A few years ago my husband and I helped start Sozo at our church. We had done a few trainings to equip and support other churches in the Netherlands. My husband and I loved it and saw the fruit of what the Father was doing in the hearts of people. We had upcoming opportunities to travel to other churches and train people in the tools of Sozo. However, in my spirit, I didn't feel like it was "hot" any longer. It didn't matter how successful it sounded, my husband and I both knew this was not what we were called to do. We could be involved in so many things that are good and may even sound successful, however, we want to focus on what we are supposed to be doing. That is our success.

The new thing for us in that season was to be part of leading a school. One portion of the school was online Bible training and the other part, that Huub and I would lead, was evenings of worship where students could encounter His heart and be activated in the prophetic realm. Every Sunday evening we gathered gave the students a place to learn to hear His voice for themselves and others, letting His words shape and transform them to His truth. It would also be a place of discovering their passions and purposes. Our heart is to equip, encourage, and empower leaders in the church as well as those who are called outside the church. So often we raise people up to do ministry for the church, and they become so busy they don't have time to fully affect their realm of influence. Our heart and goal is to provide a safe place where people can be activated in their unique gifting and be empowered and launched from a place of family and community.

Are you still wondering about the old eggs and what I did with them? It was hard for me just to throw the eggs away. What a waste it would be. I said to the Father, "So I'm just supposed to throw them away?" He said "No, put them in the recycling bin GFT." GFT in the Netherlands stands for vegetables, fruits, and garden and is used for compost. I realized that everything Huub and I did was going into the soil of the Netherlands. It wasn't for nothing. And in the soil, beautiful things will grow.

Do you know what it looks like when something has expired in your life? Do you know what you are meant to do presently and what you may need to let go of? Ask the Father what your focus should be. When He shows us things we need to let go of, we should not feel like we are being punished or that He is taking something away from us. The truth is He is freeing you up for what is coming! He has something new for you! As you let go of the expired tasks, He will bring others to fulfill that place, giving them an opportunity to grow. You can be excited about it for them and for yourself. Success is doing what you are supposed to be doing.

Measuring Success
One day I was speaking in front of a group, and I gave a prophetic word. What I shared did not have the impact I thought it would. Only half the people in the room seemed to respond to what I said, while others looked like statues. I asked the Father afterward, "What happened? I really thought I was supposed to give that word of joy." He said, "You did so well!"

How do you measure success? Is it in the numbers? Is it by how many people respond to you as you speak? Or how many people come to you after you speak and tell you how well you did? These measurements can trip you up and slow you down.

I realized at that moment that sometimes we release something small, seemingly insignificant, that starts a movement. So many tiny activities in the earth become great movements. Melting snow from a high mountain in the warm of spring starts off with tiny little drops, then the drops become a trickle, and the trickle becomes a stream, and the stream becomes a river. The small drops start something. They start a movement.

This movement increases and joins with other movements and rivers. And as the rivers find each other, they connect and flow into a large body of water or ocean. We are those droplets that start movements. As we reveal the Father and cause creeks to flow into streams and streams to flow into rivers, the earth will be filled with the knowledge of His glory just "as the waters cover the sea" (Hab. 2:14). Every drop you invest matters. You are creating a movement.

Have you ever been speaking in front of an audience and felt like some people were completely lifeless, looking like statues? The truth is, we have no idea what is going on in their minds. Many times while speaking I've come across people who, on the outside, looked as though they were disengaged. I have held meetings where it seemed like nothing was happening, but I continued to focus on the Father, releasing what I believed He was saying and doing. After the message, those same people have come to me to tell me how impacted they were. One time, a man sat at the very back, with his arms crossed, looking angry throughout the entire service. Afterward, he came to me to tell me that he hadn't wanted to be at church that day, but what was shared deeply impacted him. I was shocked. What I imagined an impact to look like is not what I saw happening with that man. My husband and I prayed for him. He came back to us weeks later and said everything changed for him and went into detail.

How should we measure success? After I speak or do anything, I practice asking the Father how we did. All the other measurements— the outward expression of receiving ministry, people coming to me afterward—could be misleading. I do not wait to hear how many people tell me I did well to be assured I had an impact. That is all great, and I appreciate that. However, I wait and listen to hear what the Father says about how we did. As He shares with me how we did, I bask in that. I no longer need to entertain people to get a response. I am not here for me; I am here for them. I can only lead them to the water; I can't make them drink. That is their responsibility.

I also value receiving constructive feedback from people if they have ideas to make what I do better. I like to hear it. Feedback should be a gift. However, the Father's feedback is the most important to me. His thoughts always cause me to go forward no matter if it was positive or something I could change. He is my gauge and focus. I don't want my focus to be on what people want, but rather on what God wants, because I know the Father has the best for them.

You are who you are—with or without your title. Have you ever thought about people who step down from ministry or leadership and move to a new location and a new profession, starting over where no one knows that they were once called pastor or elder or director? Are they less valuable than they were? Has anything changed with who they are? No. We are called to be who we are, regardless of where we are and regardless of our title.

Don't let a title define who you are, but rather let the title be a reminder of why it was given to you—to impact people's lives. The title doesn't make you become what the title is. Your life should speak for itself, and who you are should be obvious to people regardless of whether you have a title or not. Be who you are, and that will speak louder than any title. Too many people wait to be given a title instead of being themselves. Success is achieved when we can find our identity in who we are and not our title. Who are you? You are His Beloved! The one He loves—His dear, cherished, and treasured one.

Activation: Let His Words Define You

Let His words define you. Ask the Father, Jesus, or the Holy Spirit the following questions:

1. What was your dream about me in the beginning?

2. What is important about my role in life?

3. Is there a lie I believe about myself? What is the truth?

4. Is there a lie I believe about my role in life? What is the truth?

5. What do I need to believe about myself?

Now take a moment and allow yourself to dream, asking yourself the following questions:

6. Why do I give my services, gifting, and/or talents?

7. What is the message I want to send?

8. Why am I doing what I do?

9. What is the end result I want to leave behind?

10. Once I've achieved my dreams, what happens next? (Allow yourself to dream about it.)

CHAPTER 4

ON THE SAME TEAM AND ADVANCING THE KINGDOM

You are part of this great movement that is here now and ever increasing: this great movement of His sons and daughters arising and shining. However, there are enemies and adversaries that come against the movement and our ability to arise into greatness. One of the worst enemies of this great movement is not realizing we are on the same team. As Christians, we believe we are one body, family, and community—we believe we are all on the same team. However, in the churches around the world, competition, jealousy, comparison, and insecurity destroy what we are building. They come and rob our hearts and minds, disconnecting us and causing us to withdraw from one another. We become concerned with losing our place, believing our role is not necessary, or thinking that others could do it better. These lies have caused us to stop and not take ground. When we buy into these lies, our impact is weakened, and we subtly withhold our support from others.

I am convinced that the more we believe in and support one another, the greater the impact we will have. If we are truly about our Father's business, about advancing His Kingdom and increasing this movement, we must fight back, shut our eyes and ears off to the lies being shot toward our hearts, and focus on the vision and success He has prepared for each of us individually. We must press forward, advancing and shifting our focus to the reason we do what we do. As each person walks in the greatness of who they are, being carriers of His goodness and impacting their realms of influence, our lives will display what living in the reality of being seated in heavenly places looks like—bringing heaven to earth wherever we are. Dream about that for a moment. Let us also see it with our own eyes, playing out as reality on earth. You and I get to be part of the greatest movement that is here and ever increasing.

For me, the reason I do what I do is to impact lives. I intentionally give myself so that each life is transformed and comes into an encounter with God's heart, His love. That's my focus. I have the choice all the time of where to put my focus, especially when I have thoughts of comparison: worrying about someone taking my place, not feeling significant or recognized for something I did, being compared with someone who has a similar gifting, or feeling like I am being hidden while someone else takes the credit. In those moments I shut my eyes and shift my focus on my goal and reason for doing what I do. I shift my focus to make sure I hit the mark, aligning my heart with His and expressing God's heart for each person, each gathering, and each situation. Then I intentionally wait to receive what the Father says about me in those moments as I receive my significance and celebration.

Let's look at some amazing leaders in the Bible who could have had a greater impact if they would have stopped and dealt with enemies of competition, jealousy, comparison, and insecurity.

Joseph's Dream

> When his brothers saw that their father loved him more
> than any of them, they hated him and could not speak a
> kind word to him. Joseph had a dream, and when he told it
> to his brothers, they hated him all the more.
>
> (Gen. 37:4–5, NIV)

Joseph shared his dream with his father and brothers. Receiving
dreams and visions from God was normal because immediately
his father and brothers knew the interpretation of the dream:
Joseph was going to be in a position to rule. Before Joseph shared
the dream, he had already experienced hate from his brothers
because of his father's favor. It is possible that the situation would
have been different if he had used wisdom in sharing the dream.
It is important to have wisdom in sharing any revelation you
receive.

However, Joseph's dream was from God, and in the end, we
read that it came to pass. Later, his interpretation of Pharaoh's
dream, revelation, and wise plan for Egypt saved his kingdom and
his entire family, as well as the surrounding kingdoms. Joseph's
brothers and their nation needed the dream to come to pass.
They needed Joseph to succeed and be in the place to rule and
govern.

Isn't that what we want to have happen in our lives? Isn't that
what we want to see in the world around us? Seeing our God working in power and demonstration, releasing wisdom and revelation
through us—all that will save and change lives, families, communi-
ties, nations, and the world?

Yet, Joseph's brothers hated him because they knew that their father loved Joseph and favored him more. Hearing his dream of ruling and being great made them hate him all the more. It is true; we all have a need to be loved and recognized. What can we do when such insecurities arise? How do we react when those insecurities are instigated by our experiences from the world around us or by our experiences with our earthly parents or spiritual father or mother?

Joseph's brothers had a choice to either deal with the root of their insecurity or get rid of their obstacle by killing their brother. But what if they had succeeded? What would have happened to their family, kingdom, and surrounding kingdoms? That thought alone empowers me to take my thoughts captive and get to the root of any insecurity that tries to take hold in my heart. Thankfully we have Jesus Christ that lives in us. We have continual, unbroken communication with Him—we can connect and communicate with Him, asking Him what lies we believe about ourselves and how to forgive the ones who perpetuated that lie and receiving all He has for us in return.

What would have happened if Joseph's brothers had connected with God? Perhaps their story would have ended differently if they had involved Him in the situation, saying "Father God, You know we are jealous of our brother because our father favors and loves him more than all of us. We need You! Will You fill us with Your love? Father God, what is the greatness You see in us? Will You set people in our lives who will love us? What do You love about us?" Just imagine if they had sought healing and love instead of hatred and revenge. God's love would have overpowered all of their insecurities, calling them to greatness. If they had dealt with their insecurities and received love, it would have changed history. What would history have looked like?

When we have a hard time allowing people around us to be great, it is often because we ourselves do not feel significant, loved, or accepted, and we compare ourselves to them. It is so important that we get our love from the source that never runs out. That is the only way to truly deal with insecurity. When competition, comparison, or jealousy arise, we have a choice: we can believe the lies that we are insignificant, or we can go boldly before God and invite the Father to lavish you with His truth and love, letting His love and truth define us.

Take time to do this even now. What pain or insecurity have you felt or experienced recently? Perhaps there is still pain of feeling unloved from years past. Ask God these questions: What do You love about me? What is the greatness You see in me? Give Him any pain you've experienced from others, and wait for Him to speak to your heart. Receive what He gives you in return. What do you hear, sense, or see? Write down the first things that come to mind. When you experience His love and truth restoring and healing your heart, you will know that you have heard from Him. Give yourself permission to receive, and let it deeply penetrate your heart and spirit. As your mind and emotions are renewed by His truth and what He has in store for you, allow yourself to replay that encounter over and over, like it is the first time you are experiencing it.

For too long the church has ignored the presence of insecurity, letting it remain by buying into its lies that we should not need recognition, love, or encouragement because we have died with Christ. These are lies! Your old self did die with Christ, but now you live in His full, resurrected power and love. The same love that the Father has for Jesus, He has for you (John 15:9). That truth alone should change your perspective of who you are and what is available to you!

It is time for the church to get rid of these false ideas so we can fully receive love and recognition in every situation that comes up in life. Then we can be radiant, shining in confidence, and be all that we were created to be! I believe He placed this thirst and desire of love, significance, recognition, and need to be celebrated in our lives as an invitation to live and abide in Him, where He supplies all our needs. He is the One who will love us perfectly. He always calls out the greatness in you because He created you and wired you for a great purpose and destiny. And you get to enjoy it, with Him being there every step of the way. Aren't we so rich with Him?

Joseph's brothers needed Joseph's dream to come to pass—they needed him to be great. In the same way, we need everyone's dreams that are from God to come to pass. It is vital and necessary! We are on the same team. We need to stop anything that would cause us to draw back from one another, learning to connect and support each other, not only in our outward appearance, but also with intention and sincerity. As we do this, together we will have a greater impact with an unstoppable momentum. We will indeed see the sons and daughters revealed, covering and filling the earth with His goodness and the knowledge and revelation of Who He is.

Nothing Can Stop Him
What I love about Joseph's dream is that nothing could stop it! His brothers were not the only ones who tried to stop Joseph's success. After Joseph rejected Potiphar's wife, she tried to frame him and had him sent to prison (Gen. 39:7–23). All the while, Joseph kept his heart pure before the Lord and nothing could stop God's plan from coming to pass. When we walk with God, living in relationship with Him and stewarding everything He gives us, nothing can stop the plans and dreams He has for our lives. I've held on

to this truth, which has allowed me to rest in circumstances that would have otherwise provoked me to insecurity, fear, and even self-promotion. I am convinced that He will promote me and get me wherever I am meant to be. I am convinced I am not only carrying out my dream but His dream too. It is His great pleasure that I succeed, being His dream come true on earth. He desires that every vision and dream comes to pass; He gave them to me for a reason; they're not only mine, but they are His too. In like manner, you carry the visions and dreams of His heart, and it is His great pleasure that you succeed.

Advancing the Kingdom

In 1 Samuel 17, David killed Goliath. Aware of David's great success, Saul began to send him out on missions. Whatever mission David was sent on, he succeeded in advancing Saul's kingdom. So Saul set David up for success by putting him in the right position to have the greatest impact as a high officer of his army. David and Saul were on the same team, right? They were working well together advancing the kingdom until something happened.

When the men were returning home after David killed the Philistine, the women came out from all the towns of Israel to meet King Saul, singing and dancing with songs of joy on musical instruments. They were having a joyous parade. As they danced, they sang:

Saul has slain his thousands,
and David his tens of thousands.

(1Sam.18:7 NIV)

At that moment Saul stopped seeing David as an ally and a teammate, and suddenly David became a threat. In order to uphold his status and remove the competition, Saul had David removed.

With David on his team, they were both great and advancing the kingdom, causing everyone to benefit from the victory. In reality, they were both winning. But Saul lost sight of that in his jealousy and insecurity.

Saul was being compared to David. I can understand how this could have upset Saul. Who enjoys being compared to someone else or having their victories belittled? It is vital to be careful how we talk about one another. We should not compare one's greatness or victories to another. We often lose sight of what matters when we are compared to others. In moments like these, we need to recognize that we are on the same team. We do that by shifting our focus from ourselves to our greatest goal and vision: advancing His kingdom so the earth will be filled with His glory. If Saul had kept his focus on what really mattered, he would not have wasted his time trying to get rid of David. Together they could have had an even greater impact. They could have been unstoppable and had an ever advancing and increasing kingdom.

Similar Gifting

It is easier to embrace each other when we have different giftings. We recognize much more quickly that we need each other because we feel supported in our weaknesses and secure in our strengths. However, when we have similar giftings, that's when people tend to feel threatened and begin to compare. Saul and David had a similar gifting. They were both victorious in battle and were both to be great leaders and chosen to be the king (1 Sam. 11:6–14, 1 Sam. 16:1–13).

Saul was afraid that David was going to take his place as the king. He took the bait from the enemy, believing the lie that he was not on the same team as David and that David was a threat to him. When our gifting is similar to another's, we buy into the lie that the other person will take our place and that we are no longer needed. This is where our definition of success becomes most important. If we understand our purpose and are confident in our role, we would stay focused on what truly matters and not get caught in the trap of comparison. You are unique, needed, and completely necessary. At the end of the day, even if a person has a similar gifting as yours, their victories are your victories because we are all on the same team.

Fathers and Mothers

Why was Saul so afraid of David taking his position as the king? While their similar gifting played a role in Saul's insecurity, there was also something lacking in Saul's vision. If he were truly after advancing the kingdom, Saul's vision would have been long term. Did he think he would live forever and not pass his throne to someone else one day? He wasn't living past himself.

God is into advancing the kingdom. No matter how hard Saul fought it, David was going to be the king instead of Saul. However, Saul failed to realize that he had an opportunity to have a significant impact on David both as a king and father. Saul had an opportunity to train David up to be an even greater warrior. He could have set David up for success as the next king by supporting him, believing in him, and loving him. Saul could have left a great legacy if he had chosen to father David toward greatness.

If our identity is in our positions or our titles, our vision will be limited to only what we can accomplish ourselves and during our lifetime. We don't take a step down when someone else comes in to fill our place. We need not be afraid of it. We should be living for the day when someone comes with fresh energy and perspective, ready to be trained and equipped to go farther than we can take them. Fathering and mothering that person becomes our greatest role. Our impact will only increase when we step up and set up the next generation to thrive and operate in their fullness. Only then will we truly advance the kingdom.

As leaders, when we believe in someone and set them up for success, they will grow up to be great. Have you envisioned what it will look like for the people you father or mother once you are gone? Do you want them to exceed what you have accomplished, pressing forward to do even greater things? There are people we are meant to believe in, pour our hearts and lives into, and even place into leadership roles, much like Saul made David chief of the army. When that happens and we have given everything we can and set them up for success and greatness and when they achieve greatness even in our lifetimes, how will we respond?

Just as Saul had a choice, we as leaders have a choice as to how we will respond to those we lead. We can either allow insecurities to separate us from them, reducing our impact, or we can face our insecurities and continue to believe in and cheer on those we lead. We have yet to take over the world with His goodness and to operate at our full potential. Our greatest role will be to father or mother others.

I believe that is in your heart and the heart of every individual to be a good father or mother and lead others to fullness. I believe this because we were created in the image of the best Father, and we get to represent who He has been to us. There are no limits in Him. He died so we can live. He is the One who said, "Very truly I tell you, whoever believes in me will do the works I have been do-ing, and they will do even greater things than these" (John 14:12). You will do even greater things. I believe it is His delight when you do! What a good Father!

An Undivided Heart

How we keep our heart before God and respond to our spiritual fathers is also vital. David displayed an undivided heart and kept his heart pure in every situation that came against him. Time and time again, David had the opportunity to take justice into his own hands and remove Saul from the picture. Yet, David recognized Saul as a father. I wonder what was going on in his head? David, being innocent and having done nothing wrong, experienced Saul not only separating his heart from him but also allowing jealousy to keep them apart and operate not as teammates but as enemies.

Thankfully we do not have spiritual fathers or mothers out to kill us. But maybe you have experienced hurt and negativity or a spiritual parent distancing themselves from you from time to time. Those experiences can be devastating—but like David, it is important that we remain faithful. David did not divide his heart from Saul. He called out to Saul with a piece of robe in his hand, proving that he had a chance to take him out (1 Sam. 24:3–15). He proved to Saul that despite what others were saying, he was not against him, but continued to serve him. How will we respond when our spiritual fathers, mothers, and mentors disappoint or offend us? Will we say negative things about them? Or will we remain faithful and not divide our hearts from them, rather pursuing reconciliation, relationship, and connection with them?

Jesus speaks of a love He has for us called agape love. This love is not based only on feelings like philia love, which is a brotherly or affectionate love and the highest form of love people can have without God's help. Agape love is the love God demonstrates for us. It is a self-giving love that gives without expecting anything in return. This love remains constant even when we are rejected. This type of love can be a sacrifice. This way of loving has little to do with emotion, but the focus is love for the sake of the other person. This is the love David displayed to Saul, and it is the type of love that, with God's help, we can also choose to demonstrate.

The closer our relationship to people, the more we can feel pain from their actions and disappointments. It is vital that in these circumstances we receive an abundance of God's love in our heart. We need it! That's why we need God's help to learn how to love others for the sake of the world, living to see glory cover the earth, advancing the kingdom.

In Psalm 57, as David hid in a cave from Saul, he dwelt in a beautiful place of refuge in the Lord, experiencing strength and love from God and living to see God's glory cover the earth. This was not just a nice sounding, poetic psalm David sang; it is what he experienced and encountered with God. As you read this, let it come to life as you encounter who the Father will be for you in the situations you face, enabling you to be strengthened, and keep your focus on seeing His glory cover the earth.

> I will take refuge in the shadow of your wings
> *until the disaster has passed.*
> I cry out to God Most High,
> to *God, who vindicates me.*
> He sends from heaven and saves me...
> God sends forth *his love and his faithfulness...*
> Be exalted, O God, above the heavens;
> *let your glory be over all the earth...*
> My heart, O God, is steadfast...
> I will sing and make music.
> Awake, my soul!
> Awake, harp and lyre!
> I will awaken the dawn.

I will praise you, Lord, among the nations;
I will sing of you among the peoples.
For great is your love, reaching to the heavens;
your faithfulness reaches to the skies.
Be exalted, O God, above the heavens;
let your glory be over all the earth.

(Ps. 57:1–11, NIV)

A House Divided Cannot Stand

When do we know when we are operating as one team? When we celebrate others' victories, knowing that each victory is also our own, we are functioning as a team. When we have the same goal to advance His kingdom, to advance this ever-increasing movement of His sons and daughters arising and shining and covering the earth with His glory, then we know we are on the same team. You are operating on the same team when you see that everyone is succeeding all around you. There is no dividing line between you and them. We are family and one body, and we have the greatest impact when we work together.

In 1 Corinthians, Paul depicts a healthy body as one where every person is needed, necessary, and worthy of honor. He shows our dysfunction when we think or have thoughts that others, or even yourself aren't necessary, less valuable, or weaker. Just like in our own physical body where, we need each part. Each member holds a unique and significant purpose.

The eye cannot say to the hand, "I don't need you!" And the head cannot say to the feet, "I don't need you!" On the contrary, those parts of the body that seem to be weaker are *indispensable*, and the parts that we think are less honorable we treat with *special honor*. And the parts that are unpresentable are treated with special modesty, while our presentable parts need no special treatment. But God has put the body together, giving greater honor to the parts that lacked it, so that there should be no division in the body, but that its parts should have equal concern for each other. If one part suffers, every part suffers with it; if one part is honored, every part rejoices with it.

(1 Cor. 12:21–26, NIV)

I shouldn't compare my feet to my hands. One may look less desirable, but they are both of great value and completely necessary. It is vital that we separate our view of each other from the idea of one being less desirable, of less importance, or weaker. The truth is we are indispensable. Those whose roles seem less honorable should be given special honor. Those who are in the limelight are the presentable parts. They have the opportunity to walk in such a humble way that they don't need special treatment. We are all one body—unique, functioning together for the same purpose: to live, thrive, and have the greatest impact together. When one person is honored, every person rejoices with it, understanding that the whole body is being honored and encouraged. That is a healthy body.

So Christ himself gave the apostles, the prophets, the evangelists, the pastors and teachers, *to equip his people* for works of service, so that the *body of Christ may be built up until* we all reach unity in the faith and *in the knowledge of the Son* of God and *become mature, attaining to the whole measure of the fullness of Christ.*

(Eph. 4:11–13, NIV)

Each person has been given a unique function. Some are called to the church as apostles, prophets, evangelists, pastors and teachers. They are called to edify the body and give each person everything they need in order to come to their fullness. Their role is to cause other people to arise and shine and come to the fullness of maturity. They are a gift to the body for that purpose and function.

If people are not rising and coming into maturity and fullness, I would suggest there needs to be a refocus somewhere. The body is meant to be edifying itself in love, operating out of each role and gift in love. Through love we are meant to set each person up for success so that each member of the entire body reaches a beautiful expression of who the Son is.

> Instead, we will speak the truth in love**,** growing in every way more and more like Christ, who is the head of his body, the church. He makes the whole body fit together perfectly. As each part does its own **special** work, it helps the other parts grow, so that the whole body is healthy and growing and full of love.
>
> (Eph. 4:15–16, NLT)

He makes the whole body fit together perfectly, as each part does its own special work (Eph. 4:16). It is important that we know what we are called to and what we are not called to so that we don't have a joint, ligament, or member overworked. Many people in the church get worn out from doing too many things, especially things that are not in this season for us to do. As leaders, there is a place where we need to activate our ligaments. We need to let go of things to enable another part to function. Sometimes it can be easier for us to hold on to what we started because it feels like our thing, our baby. When we don't release others into it, we act out of dysfunction and can become worn out. This also prevents others from rising into a place where they are gifted and can flourish.

The Father gave me a word for the church. He said, "I'm adjusting the body like a back. When it's adjusted it will feel better and work properly. Discomfort will persist until something changes. I'm letting the body see that it needs each other. You are not a church structure but a body operating together, seeing each member as vital and necessary. Stop seeing the church as a structure but as members of a body, a heavenly habitation where Christ is head of the whole body, His mind being the operating system, giving ideas, wisdom, and solutions."

When He spoke this, I knew our backs were coming into alignment with heaven, His plans, and purposes. We were coming into alignment with His agenda and not our own. Our agenda will fall away when we align ourselves with His mind, plan, wisdom, and solutions. Discomfort will persist until something changes. A lot of the church's focus is on structure of the fivefold. As necessary as that is, if that is our main focus, we will be more focused on five people instead of operating as a body, where Christ is the Head and each member has a role that is vital and necessary.

When our body is healthy, we operate in such a way that every person is needed and necessary. The whole body is edified, growing and building itself in love. Every joint and ligament supplies a need and a support. From this place, we have the opportunity to let go of things and let others soar doing what they are passionate about. We get to let go and realize that we can be a beautiful, healthy body that edifies and builds itself up in love as we come into our fullness.

His Dream Come True on the Earth

What would it look like if every person in every church operated as being on the same team and living as a healthy body? What if we really set each other up for success, cheering each other on and celebrating each other's victories like a feast set before us? Together we are to advance the kingdom and together we can have the greatest impact! What beautiful glorious sons and daughters He is releasing into this freedom. Let us dream about what that looks like and take steps toward it, destroying the enemies trying to rob this glorious promise from us. It starts with me. It starts with you. Arise, shine, and be revealed!

Activation: Transformed by His Truth

Spend some time with the Father, asking Him to show you His truth over specific areas of your life.

1. Jesus, is there a lie I believe about my role or function in life? If so, what is the lie? What is the truth?

2. Jesus, have I compared myself to someone? If so, what is the lie I've believed and what is the truth?

3. Jesus, will You show me what it looks like for me to live for the generations to come? Will You give me a vision that will live beyond me?

4. Jesus, will You show me why my role in life is valuable and important?

5. Jesus, is there someone who I can be empowering better? If so, how?

CHAPTER 5

LIGHT SHINES BRIGHTEST IN DARK PLACES

You are the light of the world. A town built on a hill cannot be hidden. Neither do people light a lamp and put it under a bowl. Instead they put it on its stand, and it gives light to everyone in the house. In the same way, let your light shine before others, that they may see your good deeds and glorify your Father in heaven.

(Matt. 5:14–16, NIV)

We are the light of the world. As we shine, we are a luminary on the earth, releasing inspiration and influence. This is our position, to be the influencers and inspirers in the world, positioning ourselves to receive wisdom and provide solutions to the world around us, releasing the beauty of our diverse uniqueness and qualities. Arise and shine!

A town or a city that is placed on a hill is impossible to hide. All the surrounding lands and neighboring towns will see it. You are just like the city in that you are to be seen and heard; it should be impossible to hide you. You are like a lamp that brings light to everyone in the house. No one hides a lamp. A lamp's purpose is to illuminate the house for those who live there as well as for people coming in and going out. When we turn a light on in a dark room we are able to see and not stumble around. We are able to access the things we are looking for. This is how our light should be revealed: not blindingly bright so that others can't see for themselves where they are going, but a helpful luminary, revealing the situation and providing solutions for people.

As we encounter the Father and His love for us, we shine with the same radiance that He carries. Our life is the light that shines by example. As people see the way we imitate God's love for us, every action and every expression of our relationship with the Father will speak louder than any words.

It is important to remember that this verse does not say you are a light in the church or synagogue. It says you are a light, a luminary, a person of influence to the world, to your neighbors, to your very own family. As you go into the church, of course you will be a light there. However, we have forgotten our position outside of our church. It is just as spiritual to be a light outside the church—in your home, neighborhood, city, and the world around you. It is imperative that we grab hold of this: Light shines the brightest in the darkest places.

What keeps us from not fully operating as who we are to the world around us? For too long the church has been operating on the defensive—blocking, guarding, and defending their life against the enemy. We've bought into the lies that we must work hard to remain pure and safe. The dark places remain dark because we haven't gone into those places. People who are bound in darkness are waiting to have an encounter with you—to encounter the very One who lives inside of you. People are waiting to be seen and called forth into who they truly are.

Now is the time for us to be gloriously on the offensive. It is time for us to be motivated and moved by passion, compassion, and love, capturing God's heart for each person and chasing after the ones who are oppressed. What does this look like? It looks fearless. If we choose to be on the offensive, we can no longer be afraid of what others may think of us or with whom we can or cannot associate. Jesus sat with the sinners and the tax collectors. Do you think it is spiritual to eat with the "sinners" in your community—the very ones your Christian brothers and sisters may criticize you for associating with?

In Mark 2, the Pharisees ask Jesus' disciples why He is eating with tax collectors and sinners. When Jesus hears their questions, he replies, "It is not those who are healthy who need a doctor, but the sick. I have not come to call the righteous, but sinners" (Mark 2:17, NIV). Jesus wasn't afraid of what the Pharisees thought. Those sitting in front of Him were the ones that had His focus, compassion, and attention. Going to those in need was what the Father desired, and Jesus only did what He saw the Father doing.

No matter how dark the darkness is that surrounds or oppresses people, we must confidently reveal the Father's love to them, living in the reality that there is nothing the enemy can do to you because your Father is with you. Shining bright in the dark places looks fearless, bold, and undaunted by the enemy. Shining bright means acting on the offensive with one goal in mind: to set people free.

Freedom from Fear

He never leaves us or abandons us. Greater is He that is in me than he who is in the world (1 John 4:4). It is the time that we become His living word in power and demonstration. However, we must first walk in freedom from fear. When I realized I was not residing in that place of freedom in my life, I knew I needed a greater revelation of His Love for me and for the people I came into contact with.

Several years ago, I would have never told you that I had a fear of the enemy, that at one time I believed that he could do something to me—curse me or snatch me from my Father's hand. I would have never told you it was there because I wasn't aware of it myself. However, it seemed to pop up in different areas of my life. I would walk into gatherings and would sense heaviness. I could sense things in people's lives and the spirit that was operating over them and oppressing them. Instead of loving that person, I would actually remove myself from them because it bothered me so much. This disabled me from being who I was created to be and operating in the gift of discernment as an actual gift to the body.

At times, what I sensed in the spiritual atmosphere around me would be overwhelming. One day during a worship service, I heard thoughts of wanting to commit suicide, deep sadness, and turmoil. These thoughts overwhelmed me. I thought, *This is horrible! I never have these thoughts.* I knew they were not mine, but they were really intense. I understood those were not my thoughts but of someone in my proximity. At that moment, I wanted to move to the other side of the room. I realized this wrestling in the spirit was because something wanted me to leave my position. So I chose to stay.

A leader came up on stage at that point and invited us to pray for each other. He asked the congregation to raise their hand if they were going through a hard time and needing breakthrough. The lady behind me raised her hand, and I turned around and prayed for her. I declared the opposite of the thoughts I had just been having. She looked at me with tears in her eyes and said, "Wow, how did you know? I needed that so much!"

Each person is entertaining an atmosphere around them—a spiritual atmosphere built on thoughts that entertain demonic spirits and lies, or heaven and a continual awareness of God's presence. That dear sweet lady, at that time, had been entertaining suicidal and negative thoughts that created an atmosphere around her, and that atmosphere was tangible. We were given the gift of discernment to recognize these atmospheres so that we can pull people back into truth, their true identity, edifying them with God's plan and purpose for their life. It would have been the trap of the enemy if I had left my position that day. I wouldn't have spoken truth over that woman's life, preventing her from stepping into freedom and truth.

I am thankful that the Father trusted me with information about the woman's situation. I don't think the Father gives a gift that would cause me to look spiritual or for the other person to feel naked or ashamed. The gift of discernment is to be a gift to the body. Being exposed or put to shame wouldn't be a gift at all. So if you have this gift, the Father trusts you with it. Don't react to the information you're given, but wait to experience what He wants you to do with the information so that it will truly be a gift that is powerful and will have a greater impact, calling the people around you to who they are with His truth.

Sometimes when you discern something, you don't have a chance to pray for that person or you don't even know who it is for. The best thing to do in this situation is to release the opposite (the positive truth) or whatever He shows you right where you are. Pray for the situation under your breath. I pray until the burden is released and I am not bothered by it anymore. That is my indication that it is done. Then I thank the Father for it and the freedom that took place.

However, if you are discerning something and you know who it is for, ask the Father and engage with Him about the solution that person needs. Ask Him what you should do with the information, and be led by what you experience the Father doing. Operate as a gift and give His promises, truth, and freedom for the benefit of that person.

For the longest time I didn't see the gift of discernment as a gift. It seemed like a burden to sense what people were entertaining in their life: negative thoughts, new age, the occult, witchcraft, addictions. When people spoke, I would know what spirit was behind their words, or what someone was struggling with before even meeting them. Staying in a hotel or someone's house was challenging because I would discern what happened in the room as I came in. And when coming into contact with people, I would often have dreams or see flashes of images in my mind, all revealing what they were entertaining in their life. A lot of the time I didn't see this as a gift because I didn't know what to do with everything I saw and felt.

As I was learning, a lot of the time I didn't tell anyone what I was seeing but instead interceded for the individual or individuals.

I knew that the things I sensed, the negative thoughts and ideas, were not representative of who each person was and is. Rather, they were just believing lies. So I interceded and called them back to who they are, declaring what I believe the Father wanted to release in their life.

Someone came to me one day and told me that they felt like I was avoiding them. This person wanted to know if something was wrong. I knew that I didn't like the spirit that was operating over them and tormenting them, and that is why I avoided them. I also knew something needed to change inside of me. I was actually doing exactly what that negative spirit wanted me to do, which was to leave them alone, and let them believe the lie that they are rejected. I wasn't aware I was doing this, and it was incredibly uncomfortable and confronting when that person approached me. I knew then that I needed to stop fleeing and instead help them destroy the lies in their life with God's truth and love.

I realized I needed to be more perfected in love. This didn't mean that I would act out of guilt or manipulation, attending to people's every need. It meant, rather, that I would need God's help to approach those in need from a place of confidence and love. I yearned for the Father to help me. I prayed, "Father, perfect me in your love that casts out all fear, and help me to love the mess out of people's lives so that they can be delivered."

The same happened with many other people who were involved in the occult, witchcraft, or new age. I hated the spirit that they were entertaining or the spirit tormenting them. That hate was rooted in a spirit of fear, otherwise it would have compelled me to be like Jesus. Instead of removing myself from a person or a situation, I would have been moved with compassion and revealed the Father, operating in power. If fear were not my motive, it would have been easy for me to be the solution and expression of God for the people in front of me.

We need to evaluate if the hate we have toward darkness is rooted in fear. We are called to be light in dark places. We are not called to run from that darkness. When I asked God for His love to be completed in me, He started to dismantle the lies I believed and brought me into His truth. However, it was not without a cost. It is my hope that this next story I share will be like honey for you. I am the bee, producing the most delicious honey for you—the reward of never having to go through what I did to receive it.

Shifting Focus

Whatever we focus on is what we empower. Have you ever sensed the presence of the enemy or the demonic realm or seen a demon? Have you ever, in your own strength, warred against it? Did it wear you out? You don't have to war against the demonic realm in this way ever again. The truth is, we don't need to go into battle with the spiritual realm on our own. All we have to do is shift our focus to God, and He will fight these battles for you.

I dream every night. It is my training ground in life. It is a great moment when I am at rest and all I can do is receive messages, training, encounters, revelation, wisdom, and insight. In my dreams, I see people I will meet in the future, pray and intercede for people, receive encouragement for myself and others on the screen of my eyelids. It is a perfect time when I can do nothing but receive.

Every morning, almost immediately after I wake up, I write down the dream I just had, and I receive the interpretation from the Father. He speaks in the daytime and nighttime. I am convinced that He gives everyone dreams. Unfortunately, some people don't realize it, so they don't believe God will speak or simply don't understand their dream language with the Father.

I encourage you to pay attention and start writing down your dreams, even if they don't make any sense. Start going on a dream journey with the Father. The more you write down, the more you will receive. The Father loves to share His heart with you, especially when He knows you are listening and paying attention.

I am very passionate about dreams because I have been so in awe of the Father in my dream life. I could never make up what I have seen and experienced—meeting people in my sleep and then months later meeting them in person and giving them a message from the Father or receiving healing in my heart or wisdom and revelation. It is my goal when anyone shares their dream with me that they not only receive the interpretation of their dream, but also start to understand their dream language with the Father.

That's how it should be—each person becoming dependent on the Father and the Holy Spirit's revelation and interpretation, and not on a person. There are also great resources out there about what colors, numbers, and different images in your dreams mean from a biblical perspective. However, nothing trumps the correct interpretation from the Father Himself. Any spiritual gift, insight, and revelation should draw you to Him; we were not designed to operate in it apart from Him.

When you receive the correct interpretation of a dream, you should feel at peace and at rest. The dreamer should have a sense of revelation and truth, as if everything is suddenly clear. That is the indicator that a dream was interpreted correctly. If it wasn't, then the dreamer will continually search for an interpretation. They won't feel fully settled in their spirit. God designed dreams so beautifully that a dreamer will continually search until they find that peace in the correct interpretation.

I had wonderful dreams until one day the Father said, "You DO dream, and I give you dreams and their interpretation. Write your dreams down." I responded, "Yes, this is what I experience. I receive a dream, and you give me the interpretation." Then I thought, *Why is He telling me this?* Those words launched me into a season of intense dreams that lasted over six months. I experienced dreams of the enemy taunting me, and I would feel utterly alone. I would wake up sweating, with my heart beating out of my chest. I told my husband, "There is NO way this dream is from God." Thankfully, he reminded me of what the Father said, "Write your dreams down!"

In my dreams, I would go into the darkest of places. I would encounter people in a room and then discern which ones were involved in witchcraft or new age or precisely discern the places in their life where they were being oppressed. I was being trained in the gift of discernment. I could sense places the enemy was oppressing people in their body with sickness. I would point to it and could cast out the sickness.

However, sometimes demon-like people would chase me, taunt me, and lie to me. In those times, I didn't feel God's presence at all. I felt the disgusting, foulness of the enemy robbing me, and I always felt completely and utterly alone. As the demons taunted me, they said, "Look what we can do to you while your Father isn't looking." I would shout out and try to shut it all down in the name of Jesus. I would feel alone, having to fight by myself. I would quote scripture. I would sit and laugh in the face of this demon staring at me (Ps. 2:4; Ps. 37:13). I would do anything and everything I could think of to shut down the taunting of the enemy. And then I would wake up sweating, heart pounding.

After several months of waking up and praying into the late-night hours, I was completely worn out and exhausted. I finally asked the Father, "What door did I open to the enemy?" Then He revealed to me that I had a fear of the enemy. I was buying into the lies that the enemy was able to do something to me while my Father wasn't looking, that he could snatch me from my Father's hand. I believed he could curse me and take me from my Father against my will. Basically, I believed that my Father would leave me alone to fight. All the lies the enemy was taunting me with were lies I unknowingly believed.

My belief in the lies and focus on the enemy empowered his lies in my life, exhausting me even more. The Father put me on the training ground to demolish these lies in my life and reveal to me that He is strong. Whatever we focus on, we empower. My focus for too long had been on the enemy and what he was saying. Now it was time to shift my focus.

In another dream, I saw a demonic spirit staring at me. We were face-to-face. It seemed like it was over for me. I sensed the foulness of the demonic presence, and that was all I could sense. I felt utterly alone and couldn't sense God's presence at all. At that moment, I decided to stop focusing on the face of the enemy. I shut my eyes and stopped listening to what he was doing and saying or what I was feeling. I shifted my focus and gaze to my Father. "Father, you never leave me." I started talking to the Father instead. I saw this great shining light of His presence. It was like the brightness of the sun. Immediately, I woke up in His presence. I sensed His delight over me, and His pleasure that I was learning who He really is. I grew in complete confidence in Him. This was so much easier than fighting on my own! As I shifted my focus to Him, knowing He is with me, He fought the battle for me.

After this experience, I learned to operate from His Presence. He is my bold confidence and became my trump card in every situation, even in my daily life. I continued to have the dreams, and I would practice my newfound confidence and revelation. Even when I didn't feel His presence, I chose to focus on the truth that He is with me and will never leave me. My feelings were not reality, but Him being with me and for me was. When all of my struggling and warring was over, He was the One who would come and shift everything. He is our strong Father.

The dreams continued as the training continued. The enemy came and taunted me again. As I started to shift my focus from the enemy to His Presence, I heard the enemy say, "What? Do you not have enough authority to speak out for yourself?" I sank lower in humility, shrinking back from my desire to react to them. I learned to not allow anything they said to influence me. It was like I was being tested, and if I reacted to the demons, it was out of pride. I sank lower and clung even more to the Father and the truth that He was present and would fight for me. I continued to shift my focus and engage with the Father. In every situation in life, this is my reality. I don't need to be afraid of the enemy anymore. When I am tired, and I sense darkness, I rest in the confidence that the Father will give me insight and wisdom about what to do. I wait for Him to show me something or give me a solution, knowledge, and wisdom, and from that place I respond and operate.

Finally, after the six months was over, the Father said to me, "It is over! Your reward is the interpretation of all the dreams you wrote down in faith, believing and trusting in Me."

During this time I experienced the Father for who He truly is—my strong Father. He is always there whether I sense Him or not, and I put all of my trust and confidence in Him. Now I live from this place of His presence, no matter what I feel, no matter what lies the enemy is telling me. I shift my focus to the Father, His presence, and what He is saying and doing.

What will your response be when you're standing face-to-face with the enemy? Or when you're in the midst of witches and satanists? Will you give into the lie that the enemy can snatch you away, curse you, or do something while the Father isn't looking? The enemy's purpose is to instill fear and keep your focus on him. He will do anything to try to make you believe he is bigger than he is, or cause you to think he has the control and is more powerful. If we refuse to fall into his trap of lies, if we choose to focus on God's presence and goodness, we will be empowered and his work will be over. Shift your focus and communicate with the Father. He will give you what you need for every situation.

Whenever someone sees demonic spirits, I never want to hear what they look like. If I see any demonic spirits, I will not describe them to people. I will not allow the enemy to speak. They just want to instill fear that they are powerful. The Bible says that lucifer, the devil, is a fallen angel. An angel cannot even be compared to God. I never want to focus on what the demonic is saying or doing. I will only talk to the Father and see what He is doing and saying.

When we stop focusing on what the enemy is doing, we will see the Father come in mightily on our behalf. He makes a banqueting table for you in the presence of your enemies (Ps. 23). Enjoy your feast with the Father and talk with Him and ask Him how He wants to take care of each situation you are facing. Rest in Him. Ask Him to fight your battle. You'll see what He is doing and live and operate out of that reality. He is your strong Father. Cling to Him in the confidence that He never leaves you or abandons you.

Look for what He is doing in every part of your life, and watch what happens!

He Fights for Us
When we moved to the Netherlands in 2008, we experienced some opposition by deciding to live here. I got the flu, and in a moment of sickness, while Huub was holding the bucket, I heard the enemy say, "I hate you." I thought, *Um, why is he telling me this? Because, yeah, the feeling is mutual.* Huub, wanting to protect me, would go and pray around the house. We were experiencing many different things, about which I won't go into detail. However, Huub and I were tired. One night, we were about to go to the grocery store before it closed. Huub took my hands and prayed. And he immediately heard the Father say to him, "Why don't you let Me fight My battle over you?" Then Huub responded, "Father, forgive me for fighting your battle, fight your battle over us." Immediately, an angel of the Lord came into the kitchen, and Huub and I both fell to the ground. We didn't have time to say, "Look, there is an angel!" Huub hit the floor, and I fell on top of him, crying out. His presence was holy, and we were in awe. All we could do was cry out.

I heard the Father say, "Get up from Huub, I am doing something in him." I had fallen on top of him when the angel came in. It was hard for me to move or do anything, but I moved anyway, and I heard the Father say, "In this season I am training you to move even when you don't understand." And His presence came upon me strongly as we were stuck on the floor. From that moment on, everything shifted. We were so thankful to be in this place, where He fights His battles over us.

You are a bright shining light. People are trapped in the dark, and you are the light at the end of the tunnel for them—a beacon of freedom. You must take your place in love and freedom because the world is waiting for you to arise and shine. If you aren't sure where to begin, simply shift your focus from what the enemy is doing. Close your eyes to the enemy and open your eyes to God's presence. As you shift your focus, He will come rushing in with His power and solutions.

Activation: Encountering Him as Your Strong Father
Ask God the following questions. Be sure to write down what you hear Him saying:

1. Jesus, is there a place in my life where I have had more fear of the enemy than a confidence in Your power? If so, what is the lie I believe?

   Come out of any agreement with that lie, and then ask Jesus what the truth is.

2. Jesus, is there a lie I believe about Your love? What is the truth? Jesus, perfect Your love in me.

3. Jesus, who will You be for me when I go into dark places?

As you continue your journey toward fullness, I bless you to shift your gaze upon Him—your loving, glorious, powerful, strong Father! I pray over you the same prayer Elisha prayed. Don't be afraid. Those who are for you are more than those who are against you. *Open their eyes, Lord, that they may see, all the angelic army who are for them and who you will be for them in every situation they face. That they may operate from a place of rest in your presence, trusting and relying on you as they experience you as their strong Father.*

CHAPTER 6
LIVING WITH INTENTION

Your life has a purpose; you are alive for a reason. At a very young age, I came to the realization that death is not to be feared, but rather dying without fully living. Every person will die one day. Therefore, everyone dies for something. Often our lives fall into a mundane pattern: wake up, go to work, come home, eat, go to sleep, repeat. However, none of us truly want to live this way, and we certainly don't want to die this way. Imagine being found on a couch at the end of your life, with a bag of potato chips by your side, having spent your life living paycheck to paycheck and just getting by. Would that be worth dying for? What is it in your life that is worth dying for? Better yet, what is it that is worth living for? You have this one life to impact the world and the people around you. What will you live for?

I am alive today because I am to intentionally give myself to see others come to their fullness. My husband and I thrive, seeing people's hearts and lives changed. I have had glorious sleepless nights where I lay awake seeing people's faces and beautiful moments of their breakthrough flash before me. I am undone by who they are. I celebrate with the Father, saying, "Wow, wasn't it amazing when this happened in that person's life! Wow Jesus, you are so beautiful; you love people so well; you see them, restore them, and bring them back to life." I am overwhelmed by who He is as memories flash by of people encountering His love, changing in His presence, and awakening to who they are and what they carry. Seeing these moments play out continuously for hours, I weep on my pillow full of joy. I lay awake talking to Him and asking Him how we can impact them more. I ask Him questions. I feel His heart and the Spirit yearning over others. I weep over the love I experience for people, seeing them come alive! These moments I cherish. And I thoroughly enjoy these glorious sleepless nights.

One day, in my zeal and passion for what God had placed in my heart to do, I said: "Father, I will die for this!" And immediately, I heard Him say, "No, you will LIVE!" All at once I knew: we don't have to live a miserable Christian life to please Him. And we certainly don't have to carry a martyr mentality in life to truly have an impact. We are alive and have been raised up with Christ, which looks like living in fullness and resurrection power. Live out your passions and dreams on the earth. They are there for a reason. When you are living out the passions in your heart, you are fully living.

For the Joy
Part of living in fullness means discovering the joy that will carry you through life, even in the most difficult times. People have come to me and asked, "Do you ever just have a bad day? Have you had days where you just feel hopeless and sad?" I was shocked that they might have the impression that I don't have rough days. However, I saw that they were honest in their questioning, so I examined myself. I don't believe in being fake or covering up hard times with a smile on my face.

I do have hard days, just like anyone else, however I live to receive His promises over each situation. What He says becomes my reality. By remembering His promises and who He has been for me in the past becomes a launching pad of trust to face my current circumstance. Now I have a joy, peace, and confidence I live from that changes every situation that comes my way. I am in awe of Him who is faithful, who carries me through it all.

When I first moved to the Netherlands, living in another country, learning a new language, culture, and system took a toll on my body. I have dealt with migraine headaches, seeing flashes of light, adrenal fatigue, horrible digestive issues and a deep homesickness. In 2008, I experienced the Father and the Spirit yearn for the people here in Europe; He said, you are to live here. His passion became my passion. As God called me to live here, He never said that it would be easy. However, He promised He would be with me every step of the way.

In my darkest times, I had two choices: I could focus on the difficulties, or I could ask the Father to show me the joy set before me. When I was at the end of myself, I would deeply cry out to Him, "Please, show me the joy set before me. Then I will be able to press through this; I can do anything with you" (Heb. 12:2).

He began to show me the people whose lives He restored, using me as His instrument. He showed me His face, shining with delight for me, strengthening me as I realized I could live continually from that place of His delight. He showed me His dream of people arising and shining with the glory of the Lord upon them. What a joy seeing people arising, shining, and experiencing restoration, coming to their fullness and filling the earth. This is my focus when things get too difficult: this is the joy set before me. On this journey of discovery, ask the Father to reveal the joy set before you. What are His promises that will carry you through?

Strengthened Through the Storm

We all go through difficult and challenging times. David, Daniel, and Joseph, among others written about in the scriptures, had horrible things happen to them. But the Lord was always with them. There is a place from which we can live, where situations and circumstances don't dictate who we are or what we choose. There is a common lie that if something bad has happened, it means the Father has left us. This lie tries to disarm us. If we believe it, when we face a difficult situation, we will fail to invite into the situation the very One who will help us and bring about the solution.

I look for God in every situation and circumstance to hear what He has to say about it. I ask Him, "Who will you be for me in this situation? How do you see this situation? What should I believe about this person? What should I believe about myself?" His words of truth become a life-giving anchor that refreshes me and strengthens me. I endeavor to record everything the Lord says to me, whether through others or directly to me. We can quickly forget what He has said if we don't record it, allowing us to fall victim to the mind-set that He isn't speaking to us.

When I have experienced heartache, pain, or hurt in relationships, especially the ones closest to me, those have been the hardest times to sense His presence. I have been tricked into believing He isn't there, as those feelings drown out the reality of His nearness. The truth is that He is there. He never leaves us. He has made His home in us. Even in the hardest of times, that truth becomes my reality and where I live from. So I speak to Him in those moments no matter what I feel, whether I sense His presence or not. I talk to Him in the reality that He is already there, like a friend, inviting Him into my situation and giving Him the pain I experienced. In doing this, I become aware of His presence and I position myself to receive from Him.

In His presence we can find rest; we can remain in His peace that surpasses all understanding and guards our hearts and minds in the midst of the storm. As we begin to focus on His promises, His truth, and what He says regarding our situation, it anchors our souls in His reality, and brings hope that refreshes us and revives us. We are able to see the joy of His promises set before us. He gives us an empowering grace as we lean on Him and not on our own understanding.

We can live in future promises even now as we keep them set before us, reminding ourselves of them. As you do this, you empower His word to shut down every voice that tries to shake you. There is power not only in remembering His word and declaring it, but clinging to it as the truth and believing it no matter what you experience. His truth and promises become our peace in the midst of the storm. You can live and remain there. Rest in His promise that carries you into its fulfilling future.

Trust

Do you enjoy flying? I used to be afraid to fly, and I am sure I am not alone. I remember traveling from the United States to Europe by myself, as we hit some turbulence. I can handle turbulence— little bumps here and there are fine. However, this turbulence was the kind that caused the plane to drop. It reminded me of the carnival ride where you can put a penny on your knee and as you drop straight down, the penny stays suspended in midair. I could feel my stomach turn. It was dark, and I couldn't see anything outside. I had absolutely no control over the situation—I was just along for the ride.

I looked around to see if anyone else was panicked. Everyone seemed mostly calm, and then I began to wonder if the captain would even tell us if something was wrong. So I started talking to the Father and said, "I believe you said I should go to Europe. I thought you said I would arrive safely." Then I heard Him clearly say, "You will arrive safely." When He spoke, it released a tangible peace. However, right at that moment, the plane dropped again. "Father, I thought you said I would arrive safely!" I popped my head up to look around, inching myself up a little from my seat to see if anyone was in a panic. I tried to see where the flight attendants were and to catch the look on their faces. I could feel His tangible peace start to lift. He covered me with His peace that saturated me only as long as I would remain in it.

I said, "Father, if I am to arrive safely, can't you just make all this stop?" He said, "Nothing changes. If it continues or ends, you will arrive safely." I realized I had a choice: I can cling to His truth over this situation, experiencing His tangible peace, or I can pop my head out of that peace and start trying to figure things out on my own.

I am convinced that as you look for Him in every situation, He will provide what you need, whether it is wisdom, solutions, revelation, peace, hope, promises, or connecting you to the right people or places. With God, things start falling into place even when they look chaotic, scary, and painful. Cling to Him, being convinced that He has never left you. He doesn't leave you to figure it out on your own. You are in this together.

He is your best friend—the one you can trust to always be there for you. Remember His faithfulness and what He has done in your life no matter what your eyes see. Let His continual faithfulness cause greater boldness and confidence that He will do it again. Don't be like the Israelites who forgot and doubted (Exod. 16:3), but remember who He has been so that you will be launched into greater faith that He will do it again (2 Cor. 1:10). It is His great pleasure to give you the kingdom (Luke 12:32). His plans are to prosper you, give you hope and a future (Jer. 29:11).

Lightening the Load

When we want to fully live and step into our fullness, we need to free ourselves of any excess baggage we've picked up along the way. If we don't recognize what that excess baggage is, whether we picked it up knowingly or not, it weighs us down, causing our journey to be harder than it needs to be, causing us to get tired and survive rather than thrive.

I was in a season of learning that He is my good Father who knows what's best for me before I do. One day, I saw myself in the spirit like a racehorse running at full speed, focused and full of passion. I was free, doing everything that He put in my heart to do. I was running at full force! How could I not? This is what I lived for! I saw in the spirit that He was pulling the reins on me. *What?* I thought, *Why is this happening?* It was very difficult to accept. He said, "You need to know what season you are in—a rest season or a run season." Evidently, I was in a rest season. However, I didn't know what that looked like.

At that time, I was at the end of myself. My brain was so stimulated at night, it was like someone was pumping adrenaline into my body. I was exhausted and couldn't sleep. The feeling that my body couldn't keep up with me frustrated me. I have a very strong and determined mind. I can do anything I set my mind to. There is no situation I can't get out of. This is a great strength that causes me to see the possibilities in difficult circumstances. Thoughts that I could do anything I put my mind to were being tested, as I needed to embrace this body that I felt held me back.

Being in a season of rest was no longer just a good idea, it was *the* idea. God said, "If you do not take your rest in this season, the movement that is coming will be short-lived." He had my attention. I knew that I was to cancel anything that caused me to overexert myself. I was to cancel meetings or not attend them. I told Him, "But I can't just not attend these leadership meetings." He said, "If you can't cancel the meetings, then that's a problem." I later realized I was taking on too much responsibility. Conversations we had in those meetings kept me up all night long. I had to learn to let some things go.

The Father told me, "You are in a rest season until you love to live here." This was hard for me. I do love the people in Europe; however, I didn't feel at home here. My house was my little peace bubble. Every time I would take a step outside, I would be immediately confronted with the reality that I was in a foreign country. My house was the place where I could hide away and close the door to the confrontation of living in another country with my family far away. I pushed those feelings down because it is what it is; this was my way of surviving. However, God wanted me to truly live!

There were other things I pushed down inside of me that I needed to deal with, such as fears that came from living in another country. What about us having children here? I needed to grieve the feeling of loss of friendships and feeling the distance from my family. Basically, He was showing me I needed to lighten my load for the journey we were on. So I made a list of everything that would weigh me down. I would sit on the couch and deal with these issues, even the issues for which I could never see the hope of a solution. No matter how difficult they were, I faced it. I am not a victim of any circumstance.

I invited the Father into every thought, fear, and memory and let Him heal me. I waited for His promises over situations that went deep into my heart. Afterward, things didn't cost as much energy internally anymore. At the time, I had no idea how much I was carrying around. When He pulled on the reins of my life, at that time I didn't understand fully what He was doing. However, in the end, I felt so seen and loved by Him. I see Him truly loving me for me.

He wants us to live in our fullness and no longer carry issues in our life that add an unnecessary burden. He wants you to be truly free! He cares about every detail of your life! He sees you and loves you just for you. If there are areas of your life where you feel stuck, don't allow it to stay that way. Talk to the Father, make a list, and invite Him to heal each area of hurt or fear. There are also many great places to go for inner healing. I have experienced great freedom through both Restoring the Foundations and Sozo, two incredible inner-healing ministries.

Facing the issues that keep popping up in your life and letting the Father heal you in the deepest way will lighten your load for the journey ahead. Stepping further into freedom changes everything, including how we connect with people, family, relationships, and how we connect with the Father. It's time to lighten the load so that we can fully live.

Living from Passion
I am deeply moved by Paul's passion and love for the church. He lived intentionally—loving, praying, imparting, encouraging, and giving himself for the church. He gave himself for the body so that we would come to full maturity. He longed to impart spiritual gifts to strengthen the people in the churches he traveled to. In scripture he calls the people he ministered to his beloved (1 Cor. 4:14).

Paul spoke to the core of who they are, affirming their identity as saints and beloved sons and daughters of God. When we read a little further in some of his chapters, we see that the churches in various cities were falling prey to idolatry and many other sins. Yet Paul continued to call them saints and beloved (Eph. 1:1; 2 Cor.

heart and...God can testify how I long for all of you with the affection of Christ Jesus.

(Phil. 1:3–4 and 7–8, NIV)

For this reason I kneel before the Father, from whom every family in heaven and on earth derives its name. I pray that out of his glorious riches he may strengthen you with power through his Spirit in your inner being, so that Christ may dwell in your hearts through faith. And I pray that you, being rooted and established in love, may have power, together with all the Lord's holy people, to grasp how wide and long and high and deep is the love of Christ, and to know this love that surpasses knowledge—that you may **be filled to the measure of all the fullness of God.** Now to him who is able to do immeasurably more than all we ask or imagine, according to his power that is at work within us, to him be glory in the church and in Christ Jesus throughout all generations, for ever and ever! Amen.

(Eph. 3:14–21, NIV)

This is why we do what we do—that all people would be filled to the measure of all the fullness of God. What would that look like? What would the church look like? What effect would that have on the world? What would every industry look like? Our purpose and our passion in life must be greater than ourselves if we actually want to have an impact. To advance and expand His Kingdom means living with intention and inviting others into a life that is full and rich. That sounds like heaven on earth to me, and a legacy I would love to see last throughout all generations.

Ministry with Intention

The Apostle Paul's heart and passion for people compelled him to travel and minister all over the land. He kept relationship with the churches he visited and remained intentional in his involvement with their daily lives. Nothing stopped him. He underwent beatings, stoning, dangerous travel conditions, bandit attacks, and criticism from fellow Jews and Gentiles. Through it all he faced the daily pressure of concern for the churches he visited. His passion and love for the people compelled him to continue. He lived and died with one purpose: for people to come to their fullness.

I'm not saying we must face such drastic challenges in order to live with intention. Some people do. However, how often do we get a little tripped up with lesser things than what Paul experienced, being offended with one another or being afraid we'll loose our position? Paul's intentional focus in ministry awakens me to a different demonstration of what it really looks like to give myself fully and intentionally for something. Paul demonstrates an intense focus, a goal that we can all attain that can compel us to never to give up and to not be distracted by anything that comes against us. Like Paul, we too can stay focused and live out of the passion of why we do what we do. As our eyes shift from ourselves to having an impact, to living for a purpose instead of living from a title or a role, then what you carry and give yourself for on this earth has a chance to remain and live on even after your life.

Who serves as a soldier at his own expense? Who plants a vineyard and does not eat its grapes? Who tends a flock and does not drink the milk? Do I say this merely on human authority?…If we have sown spiritual seed among you, is it too much if we reap a material harvest from you? If others have this right of support from you, shouldn't we have it all the more? **But we did not use this right. On the contrary, we put up with anything rather than hinder the gospel of Christ.**

(1 Cor. 9:7–8 and 11–12 NIV)

Paul's heart in this scripture grips me. He chose not to receive from churches in order to not hinder the spread of the gospel. I don't believe we all have to live like Paul did. Too often the church struggles with a poverty mentality—the idea that we have to live continually in lack. Paul didn't have to live in lack, but he chose to. In a radical move, he chose to go without—naked, cold, and starving. However, there were what he called "super-apostles" (2 Cor. 11:5; 2 Cor. 12:11) that were taking from the churches and being puffed up in their knowledge and spirituality. He intentionally made his life a demonstration of the marks of an apostle by demonstrating what a father looks like.

What I want is not your possessions but you. After all, children should not have to save up for their parents, but parents for their children. So I will very gladly spend for you everything I have and expend myself as well.

(2 Cor. 12:14–15 NIV)

Paul is a true father, and he invested himself entirely for the people he ministered to, living for them to come to their fullness. He lowered himself in order to elevate the people to whom he ministered. Isn't that what we are called to? We become a launching place for others, setting them up for success and empowering each person to come into their fullness. For each person, operating in this looks different, depending on his or her realm of influence. Whatever that may look like for you, the goal is still the same. We have much to learn from Paul and his willingness to invest himself fully for others. This is the mark of a true father and the heart for the church to embrace, that we would fall in love with His sons and daughters even more, giving of ourselves for them. As Paul demonstrated, let whatever we do, ministering from one place to another, speaking, etc. be driven by love and passion for those people to come to their fullness.

It is a dream of mine to generate more than enough income to invest in other people and their vision. As Christians, we are meant to be a people who have the greatest impact in our cities. We should not be looking for handouts, but instead experience richness in every area. The body should be the most generous of donors and a blessing to their city and state. We need a shift in our mind-set and different focus on how we can invest and generate income so that we can leave an inheritance, not only spiritually but also financially. I am convinced we can be like Paul, demonstrating the father and mother heart of God while being financially stable and abundantly generous. We do that by carrying that same passion Paul lived with. He lived for a greater purpose than himself, and it was his purpose and the One he served that defined him.

Activation: Receive Strength and Joy
Ask the Father, Jesus, or the Holy Spirit these questions:

1. Father, will you show me the joy that is set before me that enables me to endure anything. What does that look like?

2. Jesus, who will You be for me in this situation I am facing? What promises do You have for me in this situation?

3. Jesus, will You show me any excess baggage that I'm carrying? (As He shows you what this is, give it to Him and

ask how He wants to heal you. Allow Him to take you on a healing journey. If you feel stuck, like I said before, there are great places you can go to receive healing. Enjoy your greater freedom, thriving instead of surviving.)

4. Jesus, as I'm believing in and empowering others, how do You see me? What is significant about what I carry?

Blessing

As you read this book, I bless you with an even greater passion for the people you are called to influence and impact. I pray that love and passion would compel you to continue on your path, and that you would live from a place of overflowing joy. Nothing can rob you of the joy that He has set and is setting before you. I bless you to live from the reality of the promises He gives you in every situation. Let His rest carry you straight into each promise. May the Father highlight areas in your heart that have held you back and release a grace that empowers you to overcome anything, in Jesus' name. I pray that you hear what God says about you, and that His truth separates you from who you are not. I bless you to be you and to be fully alive! Come into the fullness of who you were created to be, and let passion, love, and God's encouragement be your fuel, in Jesus' name. Amen.

CHAPTER 7

THE FEAST WE FEAST ON: EXPERIENCING CELEBRATION

You need to be celebrated, encouraged, believed in, recognized, and valued to come into your fullness. You should daily experience your great significance. Unfortunately, this isn't always our experience in life. So where can we receive this celebration and encouragement? There is a feast of empowerment set before us that we all have access to; we simply need to recognize there is a feast set before us and experience what has been made available to us.

When we experience that we are not celebrated, recognized, seen, valued, important, or needed, it can cause us to a react in a negative way. Some of us, knowingly or unknowingly, try to prove ourselves by working harder or performing better. Sometimes we self-promote and at other times we withdraw, failing to recognize the value of who we are and what we carry. Some of us even desire to stop what we are doing, thinking we aren't good enough to be doing it. For others, having plowed and pioneered so long, taking ground, standing strong no matter the circumstances or blows we've endured, we are now exhausted, and the idea of quitting sounds so desirable, giving us relief from it all.

Rather than conforming to these familiar reactions, I want to take you on a journey to experience your celebration, recognition, and value—a journey to being the best version of yourself. Be you in all of your beauty and glory. Be confident in who you are—not drawing back or pushing yourself forward to prove yourself—but live out the passions in your heart.

The desire to be celebrated, recognized, seen, valued, and significant is not a prideful or negative concept that we need to push away. These experiences are necessary to our ability to thrive in confidence and come to our full potential. There is a continual celebration we can enjoy in life, and it is a celebration of who we are and who He has been for us. This is the feast God has set before us: to be strengthened, nourished, encouraged, and believed in; to share in His joy—delighting in His creation alongside Him.

The Feast
In John 4:4–38, Jesus had a feast that His disciples didn't know about. Jesus sat down by Jacob's well and talked with a Samaritan woman. She was amazed that He talked with her because Jews did not associate with Samaritans at that time. Jesus told her everything about her life. He asked her if she was aware of the gift of God—freely given, without merit or entitlement—and if she recognized who He was; she could have asked for and received this living water to drink and never thirst again. The living water that He would give her would cause her to truly live and would be a spring welling up within her unto eternal life.

I imagine that she must have felt known and understood. He told her everything about herself. She must have wondered and hoped that He could be the One they had been waiting so long for. She told Him how their ancestors worshipped on this mountain and how the Jews claim that the place where they must worship is in Jerusalem. Jesus said there was coming a time when she would no longer have to worship on a mountain or go into Jerusalem to worship.

For years the Samaritans and the Jews had to go somewhere to meet their god, a god they didn't know, traveling long distances to a city or up a mountain just to worship. Jesus revealed that there would be a time when they would not have to go somewhere in order to worship because He came to abide in them, to be the living water they thirsted for. And that water would continually be bubbling up and would never run dry. By expressing this to the Samaritan woman, He was saying that she would never have to travel or go somewhere to find Him; they would always be connected, and he would be with her, and she would know Him.

The woman was so full of joy that she left her pot where Jesus was and told the entire town about her encounter. He had revealed Himself to her. He is the One she and her whole village had been waiting for. This changed everything for her. She could now worship the Father in spirit and in truth. It was no longer about works, but a heart-to-heart connection with all truth and sincerity. This is the relationship and connection that we have access to. He lives in you and is with you every moment. This relationship is intimate, living continually connected with Him in every moment of your life, where you have an intimate knowing of who He is while also being known by Him.

The Samaritan woman and whole village had been waiting for that time, for that moment when He would come and reveal

Himself to them. What a celebration they must have experienced! But what was this moment like for Jesus? How long had He been waiting, longing to come live and abide in them and in us, to reveal Himself? I wonder how long the Father dreamed of this moment: the bridegroom revealing Himself to His bride, and the bride finally discovering her bridegroom.

After Jesus met the Samaritan woman, the disciples returned and urged Him to eat something. However, Jesus had already eaten. He informed them that He had food to eat that they did not know about. The disciples were perplexed. They asked among themselves, "Has anyone brought Him something to eat?" Jesus revealed His feast to them, saying, "My food is to do the will of him who sent me and to finish his work" (John 4:34, NIV). Jesus compared the will of the Father to food. Food is delightful, refreshing to your body and soul. He took as much pleasure in this encounter with the Samaritan woman as a hungry and thirsty person would when they finally receive refreshment from food and drink. He saw and experienced the beauty of the works of the Father, and it nourished and satisfied Him.

If the food Jesus ate was to do the will of His Father, then Jesus feasted every moment of His life as He did only what He saw the Father doing. He had a continual feast everywhere He went, and I am convinced that we can live in that same place of feasting with the Father.

How often do we find ourselves getting tired from doing the works of ministry? I am convinced we never have to do a day of "ministry" in our lives. Jesus did ministry, but it was a delight and a pleasure to Him. He did not have to work because His ministry came from a place of passion as He enjoyed His continual feast as He encountered each person.

Jesus did not have to boast to the disciples of His encounter with the Samaritan woman and how He knew every detail of her life. He had already eaten. He had already had His feast of celebration and significance as He encountered her and knew what the effects of that encounter were. We can learn how to bask in this feast He was feasting on, gaining significance and joy from God and not the things we do. We never have to tire or grow weary in what we do. We can delight and be sustained while we see our heavenly Father revealed on the earth.

Learning to Feast
There are greater encounters we can have with the Father as we see what He does among us and through us, as we shift our focus onto Who He is revealing Himself to be. This is what it means to feast with the Father: We see Him for who He is as we experience His heart for us and for others, and we revel in the moments where His goodness is revealed in the world. It fulfills and satisfies our souls.

When I see someone receive their healing, an encouraging word, or a breakthrough, I take it in as the most delicious feast I've ever had. It is like the most luxurious steak or dessert I have ever eaten, and when I take a bite, I don't just scarf it down and move on; I savor it. I slowly savor every flavor and taste. I drink in the delight of the look on an individual's face as they encounter God. I take in each moment of the encounter and reflect on the impact it will have in their life and the lives of those around them.

These moments of seeing people encounter God are like memorials for me with the Father; they are a celebration feast, and I want to remain in that place where I eat at the table of His will being done. When I see someone receive their breakthrough in any area of life, I sit back and drink it in. He is so beautiful, loving, generous, and kind. He restores, heals, and cares about each person. He sees us, and He lavishes His thoughts on us, calling us to who we truly are. He shows us He knows every detail about each person. He overturns our problems with His promises. I am in awe of Him! And it is an honor that you and I get to be His very hands and feet, eyes and arms of love as He has clothed Himself with us.

Delighting in Him

When I drink tea or coffee, I enjoy breathing in the warmth of the vapors, letting it warm me up inside. The fragrance bursts into memories I've had while consuming that same warm beverage; memories of cuddling up with a good book, enjoying comfort, conversations with family and friends, cafes, laughter, and waking up to a fresh brew of coffee in the morning.

In like manner, when I delight in the Father, I think upon Him, letting memories flash before me of His goodness in my life and the lives of others. I enjoy the memories of when God has lavished His love on me. I revisit how He comforted me when I was overwhelmed. I experience that moment again and let the memory play out like it was the first time.

I also replay moments I heard Him speak to me, tuning my ear to recognize what that sounded and felt like and remembering how it changed me. Delighting in Him is a continual awareness of His goodness and faithfulness. It looks like enjoying memories of special moments when He revealed to me that He saw me and I wasn't aware, memories of His provision and intentional care. I delight in His faithfulness when He spoke and it happened just like He said it would. And I delight in the way He speaks straight to my heart like no one else can, deeper than any words. My delight is in the times when He showed me things before they happened, preparing my heart—times when He knew what I needed before I did.

Delighting in God also means learning to receive His delight in you. As I prepare topics and activations for the school Huub and I are leading, I often hear God say to me, "Forget the kids for a moment"—like a husband and wife reminding each other not to worry about the kids for a moment and take time to remember it's about them as a married couple first. He stops me from what I am doing to show me that He wants me for me, and I experience His longing just to be with me.

Sometimes it is hard to let go of the pressure to prepare my notes for the next day or for that very evening. However, I am overwhelmed when I realize that He really wants to be with me—He loves me just for me. Everything I do can wait as I experience His delight and bask in the beauty of who He is. It is from this place that my heart is overwhelmed with delight in Him. After a while, He shows me exactly what is needed for my upcoming gathering, session, or meeting. He just gives me a revelation; it comes so simply.

Enjoy your continual connection with the Father by taking moments out of your day to stop and think upon and remember who He has been for you. Let your memories with God replay in your mind as though you are experiencing them for the first time. When you remember Him and delight in who He is, any feeling of distance will be replaced by the reality of His nearness.

Continually Connected

I am the vine; you are the branches. If you remain in me and I in you, you will bear much fruit; apart from me you can do nothing.

(John 15:5, NIV)

Have you ever read this verse and thought, *How do I remain and abide in Him? How do I know when I've stopped abiding?* It is almost the same thing we encounter when we talk about putting on the full armor of God. Have you heard that before? I was taught to speak Ephesians 6:11–18 over and over again declaring that I had the armor of God on. After being exhausted from continually praying that every morning, I asked the Father, "When did I ever take it off?"

So how do we abide, and how do we know if we have stopped abiding? If you think about it, we are one with Him. We are continually connected to Him. He is the vine that continuously sends the nutrients we need to grow and remain alive. He is our water, refreshment, food, and nourishment. As we receive these things from Him, we automatically produce fruit. Fruit appears because we are living in the perfect condition for fruit to increase. He so lovingly cares for us and supplies all we need to thrive.

We receive this nourishment and connectedness by being aware that we truly are one with God, positioning ourselves to receive His thoughts in every situation. Like a branch receiving nutrients from the vine, you can effortlessly receive everything you need to produce fruit. What happens when you are given the nourishment you need? You come alive, are encouraged, become empowered, and bear abundant fruit!

Seeing Him

The King will reply, "Truly I tell you, whatever you did for one of the least of these brothers and sisters of mine, you did for me."

(Matt. 25:40, NIV)

I was lavishing my love on the Father in my living room one day, when all of a sudden I felt His presence strongly in the room, and I knelt down to focus on and hear what He was saying. Flashes of memories of moments when people came alive in freedom kept coming to my mind. One of them came into focus. It was a memory of a dear friend who had been coming to our gatherings.

This person shared a beautiful painting of a dove flying with its wings spread out in freedom. The dove was symbolic of what was happening in their heart. Then that same individual sang a song they wrote called "Arise and Shine," a prophetic song for our group as well as a song that expressed what was going on inside of them. After they played the song, everyone broke out in dance. As I watched this individual dance, I cheered them on, filled with delight and great joy for them. This was more than just a dance. It represented that they were arising and shining, believing what was inside of them was of great value and importance. I reveled in the memory the Father replayed for me as together we enjoyed the beauty of what took place.

I was celebrating that moment with the Father, and then He said, "Thank you for seeing Me." Those words moved me as I felt His pleasure for believing in and encouraging His beautiful, powerful sons and daughters. My eyes were also opened to the truth that everything I do for another one of His sons or daughters, I am also doing for Jesus. He lives inside of them; they are created in His image. Doing things unto God is not only when we give to the one who needs a drink and when we take care of the one who is sick or in prison. He lives inside of you and me. It is also in the way we treat each other, whether good or bad, is how we are choosing to treat Him.

All the times you have loved, encouraged, given, or supported another person, you did it unto Him. We can love on Him and each other the best when we experience His love for us, receiving it from the source of love Himself and becoming an expression of that same love for each other (1 Cor. 13:4–7).

Father, I ask that you would show them the times you saw them pour out their lives for the people around them and how it moved you, how you saw them. Even the things they do for you and others in secret, how you see it all. You are our goal and prize and the very One from whom we can receive all our affirmation.

Journals of Impacted Lives

I have many friends who've had an incredible impact on the lives of those around them, not even realizing that who they are and what they offer is of great significance. They have been part of many people's defining moments. I hear stories of how one friend or another changed the lives of people all around me—myself included—and yet they seem to be oblivious to the impact they have.

Some people go from ministry to ministry, looking for someone to recognize them. Others continue serving the same ministry for years, feeling unrecognized and unseen or unappreciated for all they do. How could that be possible? What are they looking for? Do they forget the great impact their lives have on the world around them? Perhaps you know someone like this, or maybe you have experienced this yourself.

There was a time in my life when I was in transition. I thought that I would be recognized in a certain role or recognized for the ideas and dreams that I had launched or prophetic words I had given. It seemed like the people I cared about and needed the most were withdrawing from me. I was devastated, and I needed some encouragement.

That night I had a dream. A girl came to me and said, "Look! Have you read these journals?" I noticed a huge stack of journals on my desk. She opened up one of the journals, and I saw that the pages were full of stories written in different colorful ink. These were all stories people had written of how I had impacted their lives. The journals were full of celebration. The pages of the journals were completely full, front and back. I realized I had never seen these journals before. They had been on my desk the whole time, and I had not read them. I thought, *They are all here for me to read. I need to read these.* Then I woke up.

I live to impact people's lives. Isn't that what it is all about—seeing people's lives restored, being about His business? After my dream, I started to let go of everything that made me want to stop what I was doing. I let go of the pain and hurt from past negative experiences. I kept my heart open for those around me who needed love. However, I also needed encouragement. I really did need to read the journals that I saw in my dream, to take in the moments and times when my life impacted others.

I started to document when people wrote me a letter, card, or message of how their lives had been changed. I received encouragement from the Father that would help me keep my focus when anything else came to distract me. I would read and call to memory God's encouragement when I doubted or when I didn't feel significant or recognized. Impacting lives is what it's all about. This is what I give myself intentionally for. My journals were for the Father and for me, to celebrate together. Doing this become fuel to the fire as I was empowered, celebrated, and encouraged.

I encourage you to do the same. Document encouraging cards and letters people send your way. Save the ones that touch your heart deeply. Spend time writing down what the Father thinks of you. Ask Him to reveal His truth over your life. Let it become the fuel to your fire and your encouragement and reminder when you may have forgotten that who you are is important. Start journaling and read your journals of impacted lives.

Basking in His Celebration

My Father's house has many rooms; if that were not so, would I have told you that I am going there to prepare a place for you? And if I go and prepare a place for you, I will come back and take you to be with me that you also may be where I am.

(John 14:2–3, NIV)

In a vision the Father brought me into this beautiful room. The wallpaper was made of pictures in perfect, precise layout. Each picture fit perfectly, one next to the other, covering the whole place everywhere I could look. These pictures were captured moments of victories God and I had won together.

The pictures went up all around me as far as the eye could see. There was no ceiling. I was excited with the expectation of more victories to come, filling the walls even higher and higher. Each picture had movement, playing like a movie clip of past events. As I looked at each picture and watched the memory play out, I remembered all of the life-changing and defining moments He gave to me, all of His promises fulfilled. Each picture represents memories of who the Father has been to me. He brings me to that room when I enter into worship, and it is from that place that my worship and adoration flow.

I believe He has prepared a place like this for you, a room full of memories and monuments of His faithfulness. It is a trophy chamber in heaven, a memorial to all of your victories. And it is a place where you can remember the times He delivered you, saw you, and you experienced His heart of love for you. Ask Him to show you this place He prepared for you. This is God's way of celebrating you—take time to soak it in and enjoy it!

All I Have Is Yours

Many people know the story of the lost son who sold his inheritance, and when He decided to come home, before he could say a word, his father ran out to him and restored him to the place of sonship. The son was shocked to discover that he didn't have to be a slave working in his father's house like he thought he would. He was free to live in relationship with his father, his authority completely restored to him.

At this same time, the older brother was out in the field working. When he came near the house, he heard music and dancing. There was a great celebration, and he didn't know what it was about. Then he learned that his brother had returned home, and they were celebrating his return. He was angry and didn't want to join the party. So his Father went out to meet him where he was. His father pleaded with him to come in and celebrate his brother's return.

But he answered his father, "Look! All these years I've been slaving for you and never disobeyed your orders. Yet you never gave me even a young goat so I could celebrate with my friends."

(Luke 15:29, NIV)

All those years he had been working for his father, slaving for him and never disobeying his orders. He worked to receive his father's love and celebration, gaining his pleasure through acts of service. He was a son, living in his fathers house with the mind-set of a slave. What his father said next is astounding.

"My son," the father said, "you are always with me, and everything I have is yours."

(Luke 15:31, NIV)

This story reveals our heavenly Father and His heart to restore us back to a right relationship with Him. He celebrates when the lost return. He also celebrates the restoration of his children to their true identity. He reminds us that we have continual access to Him; everything He has is yours. That's what it looks like to be a son in the father's house. The father in the story also desired to restore his older son from a slave and worker mentality to his true identity as a son. There is so much his son was missing out on as he was working so hard for his father. He could have had parties and celebrations along with his friends, living like a son in his father's house. He could have enjoyed his father's connection and nearness, if only he had been aware of it.

Your heavenly Father has made everything He has available to you. You can feast and party, full of joy in His presence. You don't have to work a day in your life for Him when you continually experience His heart and love for you. Become aware of His joy and His face shining upon you. There is nothing you can do to earn His love. You are His son or daughter. He loved you first, and it is true humility for you to simply receive it. Let Him strip away all the good things you do for Him, every role you play in life, until all that is left is you.

Activation: Feasting with the Father

Let's take some time to feast with the Father. Let everything that you do—all the roles you play in life—come off your shoulders until there is nothing left but you. Ask the Father the following questions and write down what you hear.

1. What do You love about me? (Write down the first thing that comes to mind.)

2. Jesus, is there a feast I've been missing out on? What does it look like to celebrate and feast with You?

3. Jesus, what have You made available to me that I am unaware of?

4. Jesus, will You show me a time when You celebrated me and I was unaware?

5. Jesus, will You show me a time or bring to memory a time when You saw me for who I am?

Take the time to feast with Jesus and the Father over the memories He brings to mind. I feel like some of you reading this are being healed in deep places where you have felt alone. He wants to show you that He was there in those moments. I feel like He is showing someone that you truly are beautiful, and He loves your smile. For some, He is reminding you that He saw you dance with joy in the kitchen or how you show great love to your children. He is even revealing when He saw you do something beautiful that no one knew about. He delights in you. Enjoy His delight and enjoy being celebrated!

CHAPTER 8

THE GREATEST MANTLE

Jesus said, "A new commandment I give you, that you love one another, as I have loved you, that you also love one another. By this all will know that you are My disciples, if you have love for one another."

(John 13:34–35, NKJV)

It is in experiencing God's love for us that we in turn learn to imitate both Him and His great love. This is far greater than the command to "love your neighbor as yourself" (Mark 12:31, NIV). Some people do not love themselves, let alone love their neighbor. John 13:34 is an invitation to experience the love of the Father. How can we love one another as He has loved us unless we truly experience His love for us? In fact, He is love. All we need to do is go straight to the source of love itself, enabling us to love with a far greater capacity. By doing so, we become a beautiful representation and expression of the Father on this earth.

What does it look like to be imitators of God's love? It begins with an encounter of His love for you. Then, in that same likeness, we become an encounter of love for others. Consider the various ways the Father has shown you His love. If it is helpful, make a list of all the things that reveal His heart for you. What would it look like to imitate those things you listed as an expression of His heart for others? Now, if it is difficult to make a list and your knowledge of God's love is based on what you read in scripture, I encourage you to make it a priority to experience His love. Give yourself permission to do so; it is vital for your life and relationship with Him, and of course, for those around you.

If we settle for having knowledge of God's love without experiencing it firsthand, it would be like having a marriage devoid of love-filled action and communication. What if, when my husband and I got married, we wrote a letter to each other expressing our love, expecting that anytime we needed a reminder of each other's love we would simply need to read the letter. How intimate would our marriage be? What if we never experienced holding one another, looking into each other's eyes, and expressing our love for each other saying, "I love the way you smile, you make me laugh, I am proud to be your spouse, I love that you share the secrets of your heart with me, your thoughts are so important to me." If we depended entirely on the letter to be the expression of our love, we wouldn't have the privilege of communicating the joy and thankfulness we have for one another.

Imagine yourself experiencing a daily expression of love, joy, and gratitude with your spouse, loving and honoring each other consistently with your words and actions. How would that affect your everyday life? Wouldn't everything just seem easier and happier? Wouldn't you be able to handle so much more in life? It wouldn't matter if you were rich or poor; you would be rich with each other! And what an impact it would have even on your children.

Having a day-to-day experiential, intimate connection with God is just as important as it is with your spouse. He doesn't want us to only understand His love because the scripture (or letter) tells us it is true; He wants us to experience His love and encouragement every single day. You can live a full and rich life with Him, and it all starts with positioning ourselves to receive and experience His extravagant, limitless love.

Who wouldn't want a love like this? He is the love the world is thirsting for. The more I encounter Him, the more I am transformed and become like Him. As I experience that He is a person of restoration, healing, and joy, full of delight and love, generosity and faithfulness, how can I possibly hoard that love for only myself to enjoy? I can't help but want to express that very love to the people around me. This is His longing and desire: for every person to know and experience His great and limitless love.

Limitless Love
One day when I was worshipping, I became overwhelmed with His love for me. I was thanking the Father for His love and boasting to Him about how far we had come and how I loved where I was at in life. I actually thought there couldn't really be anything more to receive, and that I could live continually like this and be happy.

Then He opened my eyes through a vision. I had my arms open wide—stretched out as far as they could. My arms were stretched out around His heart embracing it. I saw myself so happy with what I had. I was so rich with His heart, and I couldn't imagine anything more. Then I saw the picture zoom out. I noticed I only had a little piece of His heart. "Pa -Ha-ha haaaa!" I laughed out loud. I knew, at that moment, I could never say that I have arrived at knowing His love or His goodness. It is a lifelong, rich, and wonderful journey.

When we think we've arrived at knowing His love and being content to stay where we are at, then we limit ourselves from receiving more of His limitless love. Our God is limitless! I am convinced that this doesn't only pertain to His love and goodness, but anything concerning His attributes.

Each believer is a portal, a gateway, an expression of heaven and the Father, revealing what He is like and what it looks like to live continually connected with Him to the world around you. Think about who He has been for you and how you can re-present that to others. If love isn't flowing to Him or others naturally, you have a great invitation to become a great receiver of His love! The more you receive the more you can give. Love as He has loved you. Make it your priority to receive His great, limitless love for you. Isn't that a wonderful way to live?

The Greatest Mantle

I was talking to the Father one day in my room, sharing my heart with Him, when an angel entered the room. I asked him some questions to make sure he was sent from Jesus. I asked if Jesus is his Lord and if he confessed that Jesus came in the flesh. By this no Spirit can lie (1 John 4:2 and 1 Cor. 12:3). When angels are from God, they are very clear about it. I have even experienced them breaking out into beautiful songs and sounds of worship along with other angels, like an orchestra of heavenly songs. Their beautiful songs cause my heart to explode in worship as I join with them in singing to my heavenly, Heavenly Father.

7:1). He understood that their behavior didn't define their true identity.

I am convinced that when we believe in people for who they truly are and what the Father says about them, His Word, that is sharper than any double-edged sword, will cut off from them those things they are not. They will no longer identify themselves with lies that have held them captive. His truth calls them into freedom and the reality of who they are. As you read the following writings of Paul, let it impart intention, passion, and love for God, His church, and all those around you.

I long to see you so that I may impart to you some spiritual gift to make you strong.

(Rom.1:11, NIV)

For this reason, ever since I heard about your faith in the Lord Jesus and your love for all God's people, I have not stopped giving thanks for you, remembering you in my prayers. I keep asking that the God of our Lord Jesus Christ, the glorious Father, may give you the Spirit of wisdom and revelation, so that you may know him better. I pray that the eyes of your heart may be enlightened in order that you may know the hope to which he has called you, the riches of his glorious inheritance in his holy people.

(Eph. 1:15–18, NIV)

I thank my God every time I remember you. In all my prayers for all of you, I always pray with joy...It is right for me to feel this way about all of you, since I have you in my

I felt God's presence with the angel in front of me. He wore a gold helmet that masked one side of his face. He had dark-brown hair, and there was a great army of angels behind him. "We have come to punish the darkness around you. To come take authority when you speak." The angel came to me and said, "We have come to you because you are His beloved." He declared things over my life, my husband's life, and over our city, Ede, and Europe.

After the angel spoke those things, I saw that he and each angel with him had a red ribbon with a gold medal on it. It reminded me of an Olympic gold medal. The angel placed the medal around my neck and said to me, "You are His beloved." In like manner the army of angels with him came to me and did the same, saying, "You are His beloved." One after another they kept coming. Over and over again until the red ribbons, along with the medals, became thick and joined together as one. It was like a mantle over me.

This is the greatest mantle I could ever carry. This is a mantle in which I could find my identity. I wear it wherever I go. Whether I'm aware of it or not, I am continually wearing it. This is my security. This is what I sink into, relax, hope, and find joy in. At that moment I was so overwhelmed as tears of gratitude streamed down my face.

The word "beloved" is a word used for someone who is dearly loved, valued, prized, and treasured. You are His beloved! I pray you will experience life-changing love encounters with your heavenly Father! Let His love be a mantle over you. This mantle of love is the greatest, most powerful, valuable, and precious mantle you could ever carry in your life. This is who you truly are—His beloved.

For he received from God the Father honor and glory when such a voice came to him from the Excellent Glory, "This is my beloved Son, in whom I am well pleased."

(2 Pet. 1:17, NKJV)

Did you catch that? The way Jesus received His honor and glory from God the Father was through the announcement that, "This is my beloved son in whom I am well pleased." God the Father didn't say, "This is my beloved apostle, prophet, evangelist, pastor, teacher, preacher, or CEO." You also are His beloved son or beloved daughter. Let that define who you truly are. Let that be your honor and glory, and spend time reveling in what that means.

Defined by His Truth

How precious are your thoughts about me, O God.
They cannot be numbered!
I can't even count them;
they outnumber the grains of sand!
And when I wake up,
you are still with me!

(Ps. 139:17–18, NLT)

The Psalms are not just beautiful poems or lyrics that make great songs to sing. David actually experienced and encountered the things he wrote about. He experienced God's wonderful, encouraging thoughts about him so much so that he couldn't number them. They were so numerous that it would have been exhausting to count them. He even likens it to counting grains of sand on the beach. It is no wonder David trusted and relied on God. David constantly encountered and experienced God by his side every waking moment. How could he not sing his heart out to God?

David learned how to receive God's love for him, and he is a great example for us to follow. Be a great receiver of His love and thoughts for you daily. Let His words and thoughts transform you (Eph. 4:23–25). Let His thoughts even transform the situations you face. David was rich with the thoughts God had for him and was overwhelmed by them. He experienced the truth that God was with him and would never abandon him, and he knew that together they could do anything. I'm convinced this was David's confidence, his strength that enabled him to endure and to conquer whatever came his way.

We live in an even better covenant now, with unbroken communication with the Father. You have the opportunity to be overwhelmed with His thoughts for you daily, and continually. Sometimes His thoughts are too wonderful to embrace. No one has ever loved us this way before. We become uncomfortable receiving this great love that He so freely lavishes on us. It is so much easier to just keep ourselves together. Give yourself permission to think upon these things over and over, no matter what it looks like. Let His love and truth transform you. Transform the way you view yourself as you see and become who He has dreamed you to be from the beginning.

From the Head to the Heart
Have you ever received nice complements from people? You know the sort, "Oh, your hair looks nice." "Nice outfit. I love those shoes!" And it seems so superficial, so you respond nonchalantly, "Yeah, thanks…" Have you ever heard the Father give you a compliment, "I love you," or "You're my beloved son or daughter," and you responded in the same way? Perhaps it just went in one ear

and out the other? Maybe the same thing happens when He shares His promises for you. It all seems nice, but it is hard to believe. Sometimes we hear things, but we don't receive them because of our polite culture or maybe someone promised things and didn't follow through.

I remember I used to think I wasn't beautiful. I saw others as beautiful, but I was so aware of my own flaws. One day as I was driving to work, I pulled into the parking lot, parked my car, and as I stepped out I heard the Father say, "You're beautiful." I thought, *Oh, that's nice,* and I was going to continue on my way. However, I was stopped in my tracks by one profound thought: He can't lie. I sat back down in my car and wept. *He must really think I am beautiful,* I thought. His truth went deep into my heart. It changed everything for me. I suddenly saw myself differently. It was like a veil was removed, and I started to see myself the way He saw me. He thought I was beautiful, and He can't lie! These were more than just nice words or something nice to say. It was the truth.

When we encounter His truth, He transforms us, and it goes from the head to the heart as we begin to believe what He has spoken. Are there things in your life that you have had a hard time believing? He is not a man that He can lie. Revisit the things He has said or said through others. Be transformed into His truth, and let it go deep from your head to your heart. Come into agreement with Him, and receive new lenses through which to view yourself, your God, and His love for you.

His Beautiful, Shining Face

One thing I ask from the LORD, this only do I seek: that I may dwell in the house of the LORD all the days of my life, to gaze on the beauty of the LORD and to seek him in his temple.

(Ps. 27:4, NIV)

When I found him whom my soul loves; I held on to him and would not let him go.

(Song of Songs 3:4, NASB)

Have you encountered God's manifest presence? When I would hear Him speak to my spirit, I would sense His presence heavy and thick. I wondered, *Who would ever want to leave this place?* I was determined to find a way to remain in His manifest presence. Everything else was put on hold as I held on to Him, and I would not let Him go. I would not be distracted; I was absolutely determined to remain in this place. I was determined to learn how to remain. When I sensed His presence while cooking, I would run to a place where I would be the least distracted. In the middle of whatever I was doing, I would leave it, run, and learn to remain. I was zealous for that time and experience with Him. *What will He show me next?* I wondered.

One day, I was so overwhelmed with God's presence I couldn't handle it anymore. I asked Him, "Please just take me up. Please do something. I don't want to pray, speak or anything; I just want to remain and be with you." I yearned for this place like a woman who longed for her husband to come back after being away for a long period of time—a yearning so deep I had never known such a longing before with anyone.

After a while, I came to a place where I was halfway sleeping and half-awake. I felt a peace come over my body, and the Father picked me up. Like a father picks up his child, He picked me up, and I saw His face shining bright as the sun in delight for me. Joy and delight radiated from His face. I was overwhelmed with joy and love, and began pouring out worship to Him with everything within me. "I will shout it out to everyone: Your goodness! Your loving kindness! I will tell the world who you are!"

I can still see His shining face now and can play that experience over and over again in my mind. That encounter changed my life forever and has caused me to have great expectations of what would happen next. I am thankful for who He has shown Himself to be for me. However, I long for more, and that longing launches me into all that He has waiting for me.

I believe that encounter was not just for me, but also for you! I pray that you would experience a stirring up of longing and desire for the Father and an ability to remain in His manifested presence. I pray you have life-changing encounters where you experience His delight and joy over you, and experience His heart for you. You can be alive even more in His constant encouragement, as you experience His delight and face shining upon you. I bless you with one of my favorite scriptures. This scripture is an encounter. I bless you to become aware, feel, and experience His presence and His face shining upon you day and night.

> The Lord bless you
> and keep you;
> the Lord make his face shine on you
> and be gracious to you;
> the Lord turn his face toward you
> and give you peace.

(Num. 6:24–26, NIV)

He is Better than We Thought

Have you ever asked the Lord the question, "What can I do for you, Jesus?" Have you ever thought about what you can do that is truly just for Him? I often ask and ponder that very thing. I want to please Him and lavish Him with love, being so overwhelmed by the love He so lavishes on me. He loves me just for me, and I want to express that I love Him just for Him.

Let's think about that together right now. What can we do for the Father that is just for Him? Start listing some of the things that come into your mind. What can you think of? We can worship, right? However, He does have angels and elders around His throne, and they are worshipping constantly, day and night. As He turns, displaying another facet of His beauty, their worship is released all the more. In the same way, when you are worshipping and you encounter God's presence, you enter into His fullness of joy and His peace (Ps. 16:11). As we lovingly worship Him, He gives us everything we need.

If we give Him worship and He in turn gives us everything, what else is there that we can do just for Him? Read the Bible? However, is the Bible really for Him? Or is it for us to come into an encounter with who He is? The Bible encourages us and empowers us, so reading it is for our benefit.

Perhaps the thing we can do just for Him is to take care of others. He loves the widow and the orphan, and His heart is for them. He said that when you do it unto the least of these, you do it unto me. We should keep caring for the widow and orphan—He receives it as done unto Him—however, the widow and the orphan are the ones directly affected. This reveals His beautiful heart that cares about us and is moved by compassion for us as people. It also further proves and reveals His beautiful heart full of love for us, and His great delight that we are cared for. This thought causes me to be even more overwhelmed with love for who He is.

Yet, what can we do that is truly only just for Him? After continually asking and pondering this question, I am left feeling so uncomfortable that there is absolutely nothing I can give Him. Inside I feel an uneasiness, knowing I can really do nothing for Him. At the same time, there is also nothing that I can do that could make Him love me more. I wish I could do something that would cause His heart to love me more. How I desire to experience more of His love.

However, there must be something about me and my heart that He loves. That must be the very thing that I can give Him—myself entirely. What is it about me that He loves so much? Have you ever asked that question? It is a good one to ask. After you give Him all of the good things you do, all of your responsibilities, when there is nothing left but yourself, ask Him what He loves about you.

Overwhelmed that He truly wants me for me, I have decided that I will live my life desiring Him just for Him. I aim to let go of ministry and all the good things I can do, that He also cares about, forgetting about everything for a moment and lavish my love on Him just for Him. He is my joy and delight, and He is so much better than we think! You and I are on a life-long journey of discovering Him and all of His beauty, goodness, and loving kindness!

His Heart Chamber
Have you ever wanted to be the one Jesus loves most? Throughout my Christian life I have wanted to be the one that He loves the most. I would get jealous of other people when I saw that they displayed a radical love for God. I would compare myself to them. Many people say there is enough room for everyone on His lap. That idea never satisfied the longing in my heart. If we are all the same, if He loves us all the same, then no one is special. That idea caused His lap to seem so big as He increased in size and I decreased in size, until I was a speck on His lap among other specks.

That couldn't be true. That doesn't seem like a very intimate place to be, like a speck of dust on someone's lap, especially since John "the Beloved" got to rest His head on the chest of Jesus as he asked Him questions (John 13:25).

There has been this constant longing in my heart to be the one He loves most. It would pop up continually when people shared about something they did for Jesus as I listened, wishing I had come up with that idea. All the things I have been told about His love would run through my mind but wouldn't satisfy my longing. So I spoke to the Father, sharing what was going on inside of me, saying, "I want to be the one you love the most."

I waited and waited to hear what He would have to say. Then, in a vision, I saw His heart. His heart was beating for me and sweetly calling my name—Mir-anda... Mir-anda... Mir-anda. His heart was yearning for me, as He called my name. Then I saw a chamber in His heart with my name on it. This chamber was a place only I could fill and satisfy. It had my name on it, and it is where I belong. I was so happy in His heart that I went in and squeezed it, hugged it, clung tight to it. I lavished my heart on His.

In the vision, I looked outside my chamber, and there were many, many countless chambers with names written on them. He was calling out to them—continually calling out to them and yearning and longing for them to come in. I also looked and saw many of the chambers were empty. So many people have never come into this place in His heart yet. But He calls out expectantly, waiting for them to come.

You have a place in His heart, a chamber with your name on it. He is calling you home into His heart, continually, like a heartbeat. You have a place in His heart only you can satisfy and fulfill. He also has sons and daughters that have not come home yet, but with that same love, He is calling out to them, calling out to us all.

He Enrobes You

I was delighting in God's presence one day when I saw a vision of Him wrapping this beautiful white, flowing robe around me. I loved the robe; it had such great detail and craftsmanship. I was dancing around, and everywhere I went it was with me. I immediately asked, "Can my husband have one too?" He replied, "Yes, Huub can have one too." I was feeling rich, with my white robe, and joyful, yet I didn't know what it meant. So I asked, "What does this white robe mean?" and I heard in response, "Purity, worship, and humility."

The robe was so beautiful, that boggled my mind so I asked God, "Humility? Really? But Father, wouldn't true humility look like rags, or something ugly?" This robe didn't look humble to me at all. It looked and was extravagant. I felt like royalty in it, and that didn't make sense. Then all of a sudden He spoke to my spirit about a new revelation of what true humility looks like. "To be able to be truly humble, I need to see my own value and worth."

I am enrobed with beauty, value, and God's craftsmanship. He is in every detail. Now that I experience His value, and celebration for who I am, there is no need to prove who I am, let anyone else see what I did, or be upset when I'm not recognized. I know my value is from Him, and I have allowed that value to go deep in my heart. I may not ever get recognized, but I can enjoy His delight and value for me. In that I am also enrobed in purity and sweet worship to the Father.

I believe this robe is not only for me. If you want it, it's yours! *Father, I ask that you would enrobe the person reading this book with this beautiful white robe of purity, worship, and humility. Open their eyes so they can see what it looks like—the fine craftsmanship of how much you value them. Reveal their value in every area of their life.*

Forgiven
Ever since I came to know Jesus, I have kept a journal of encounters, dreams, visions, and my expressions of pouring my love and heart out to the Father. I would write down everything He would say to me. I also wrote down my prayers for other people and the things I would hear God say concerning others. Best of all, I got to watch those very things take place! It was all recorded in my journal, and I loved to be wowed by God! Forget being told to pray for an hour. I couldn't wait to see what He would do next. In one of my entries, I was telling the Father something I did that I was ashamed of. Before I could write down, "Please forgive me," He said, "You are forgiven." In my journal, that is what I wrote instead. I was overwhelmed that He forgave me before I could even write it down. I said, "Wow, Father, you are so quick to forgive!" He said, "In that same way, you are also to forgive." That one conversation with God has changed my marriage, family, friendships, and people I come in contact with. He is so forgiving to me; how can I not forgive someone else, and quickly? I was really good at this for years. Anything that came up, bam! Forgiven! I know what it is to be forgiven. So it was easy for me. I am convinced that unforgivingness keeps us in a prison cell, robbing us of life.

There was someone who was close to me in my life who really hurt me. The pain they caused was incredibly deep. After many years of the same thing happening over and over again, you can imagine that this pain was hard for me to let go of. For the first time in a long time, I felt my heart get hard, wanting to protect myself from any future pain. I pushed the thought of that person away and buried the pain and tried to move on as my heart was hardened.

The next day I asked the Father, "What do you want to do today?" He said, "Go and get a journal and read it." And as I mentioned before, I have a large number of journals that I use to talk to God and record what He is saying each day. This was all before the iPad, of course. I went upstairs and randomly picked out one of my old journals from years ago. I opened it up and on the open page, I saw, "You are forgiven." I was overwhelmed again by His forgiveness for me. He was so quick to forgive. And I read again what He had said, "In that same way you should also forgive." At that moment my hard heart softened as I experienced God's forgiveness all over again. How could I not forgive? I forgave that person, released the pain, and received from God what I needed in that situation.

Hearing Him say to me, "You are forgiven" before I could even finish my sentence made me realize how quickly He forgives us all. I have learned to quickly, no matter what my emotions, choose to forgive. I give God the pain and receive what He has for me in return. He is so good and desires us to become free. Remember the times you've been forgiven. And just as He has forgiven you, you should also forgive (Eph. 4:31–32, Col. 3:13). Represent to the world who He has been for you.

Activation: Transformed by Truth and Love
My husband, Huub, and I take all the prophetic, encouraging words, promises, and scriptures that we recognize as His truth for

us, His promises, and the words that go deep and touch our heart, and we place them all in one document. We then take those promises and prophecies and turn them into declarations. We also have a document of words and declarations specifically for our marriage. We often read it out loud over ourselves and over each other. We also have prophetic and encouraging words recorded on an MP3 player. We listen to these encouraging truths and let them shape us and define us. I encourage you to create a similar practice with the things God is revealing to you as you continue these activations at the end of each chapter. Turn His truth into declarations over your life and the lives of those you love. Be transformed by His truth!

As you ask these questions, take time to let Jesus take you on a tour in His heart. Write down what you sense, feel, and see:

1. Jesus, will You show me the chamber in your heart with my name written on it? What does it look like?

2. Jesus, will You take me on a tour of Your heart and show me Your heart for me?

3. Jesus, will You show me the delight and joy You have for me?

4. Jesus, what is Your joy? What is it in my life that makes You happy?

5. If you are going through a difficult situation, you can ask: Jesus, who will You be for me in this situation?

6. Jesus, is there someone I can forgive? (It is possible that the person could be yourself.)

Prayer: Father, I ask for life-transforming encounters of Your love! I want to see you for who you really are. I want to display who you truly are to the world around me. In Jesus' name. Amen.

CHAPTER 9

OPERATING IN THE PROPHETIC AND SPIRITUAL GIFTS

*Follow the way of love and eagerly desire gifts of the Spirit,
especially prophecy...the one who prophesies speaks to
people for their strengthening, encouraging and comfort.*

(1 Cor. 14:1 and 3, NIV)

We are to follow the way of love and eagerly desire the gifts of the Spirit, especially prophecy. It is necessary that we desire and go after the gifts of the Spirit. We are to all operate in them fully, and there are important reasons for it: equipping, strengthening, encouraging, and comforting His body so that we come to our fullness the way He dreamed us to be from the beginning. The greatest way we can do that is to follow the way of love by prophesying.

Prophecy is the most powerful way to strengthen, encourage, and comfort the body. As the Father reveals details about people's lives, they feel known and seen by Him. When we prophesy, we hear solutions, plans, and promises over people. We hear the Father call out who they truly are, and they, in turn, are transformed by that truth, from glory to glory. Prophecy is a beautiful, powerful gift.

> Now you are the body of Christ, and each one of you is a part of it. And God has placed in the church first of all apostles, second prophets, third teachers, then miracles, then gifts of healing, of helping, of guidance, and of different kinds of tongues. Are all apostles? Are all prophets? Are all teachers? Do all work miracles? Do all have gifts of healing? Do all speak in tongues? Do all interpret? **Now eagerly desire the greater gifts. And yet I will show you the most excellent way.**
>
> (1 Cor. 12:27–31, NIV)

We are to eagerly desire greater gifts for the purpose of edifying and building up each person. In the body of Christ, we have each been given a role, which for some is to fully equip each individual. That should be their focus, for the edifying of the body until we reach full maturity of the knowledge of the Son of God (Eph. 4:12). This is the beautiful reason why each person is placed in such a necessary and vital role.

There is a more excellent way we can operate out of these gifts and roles. There is a place of abundant fullness, where we can enjoy a continual encounter with the Father and with people, where what we do is no longer work. In 1 Corinthians, Paul shares that there is a more excellent way of operating from our role and gifting. This is the key that is going to unlock a historic movement for the church.

If I speak in the tongues of men or of angels, but do not have love, I am only a resounding gong or a clanging cymbal. If I have the gift of prophecy and can fathom all mysteries and all knowledge, and if I have a faith that can move mountains, but do not have love, I am nothing. If I give all I possess to the poor and give over my body to hardship that I may boast, but do not have love, I gain nothing. (1 Cor. 13:1–3)

We can operate in the greatest gifts imaginable—sharing the details of people's lives, future events taking place, mysteries never heard before, working miracles, and healing diseases. Yet, He is showing us a way that exceeds them all. If I am not operating out of a place of love, if love is not my motivation, then it is just noise in His ears, like a clanging cymbal.

This is the great invitation: to step into an even more significant encounter in all we do, living in a continual love encounter. The Father is inviting us to experience who He is for each person, leaning into His compassion and delight. We are invited to be His heavenly expression on the earth.

Love never fails. When you are operating out of love, you will never fail. When your focus is for the benefit of the person in front of you, that they come into their fullness and encounter God's heart for them, you won't fail. This is the glorious place from which we get to live: a place of fullness and continual encounter with the Father and with people.

When I operate out of a spiritual gift, I myself have an encounter. I am in awe of the Father's thoughts and plans for the person or family in front of me. I hear what He says about them and experience His heart for them. His heart moves me, and I become a demonstration of who He is revealing Himself to be at that moment. As that person receives inner healing, physical healing, and/ or encouragement, I fall more in love with the Father. I am in awe of who He is. Healing and prophetic words come easily while operating in this place of love. As we focus on who the Father is revealing Himself to be in these moments, greater encounters of who He is await us.

When Completeness Comes

> For we know in part and we prophesy in part, **but when completeness comes, what is in part disappears.**
>
> (1 Cor. 13:9–10, NIV)

One day, I read this verse with new understanding, and I burst into tears. I have always read and believed that we know in part and we prophesy in part. I always leave room for interpretation in any prophetic words I give and receive. However, there is a great revelation and promise in the final half of the verse: "But when completeness comes, what is in part disappears."

Did you catch that? There is a time coming when what we know and see in part will disappear. We are progressing forward. Coming into fullness from glory to glory. For the longest time, I believed only part of a verse. When we limit ourselves to only half the sentence, we allow the veil—that has actually been removed—to remain. I have been limited my whole life by half a sentence. However, there is a great revelation and promise in the final half of the verse: "But when completeness comes, what is in part disappears."

When Jesus came, He gave His life for us—the veil that separated us from complete access to Him was ripped from top
to bottom. "When Jesus had cried out again in a loud voice,
He gave up His spirit. At that moment the curtain of the
temple was torn in two from top to bottom."

(Matt. 27:50–51, NIV)

Even to this day when Moses is read, a veil covers their
hearts. But **whenever anyone turns to the Lord, the veil
is taken away**. Now the Lord is the Spirit, and where the
Spirit of the Lord is, there is freedom. And **we all, who
with unveiled faces** contemplate the Lord's glory, are
being transformed into his image with ever-increasing
glory.

(2 Cor. 3:15–18, NIV)

The removal of the veil brings two things into focus: who He truly
is, and who we truly are. We all have complete access to Him and
can behold His face, seeing Him for who He really is. This is for everyone, for all of His sons and daughters. We can talk openly with
Him, face-to-face and heart-to-heart.

When we practice the revelation that we can speak to Him
openly, and as we behold Him and see Him for who He truly is,
imperfect knowledge of who He is will vanish. What was in part
disappears because we behold Him, as He is revealing Himself to
us from glory to glory and from encounter to encounter. The veil
that has restricted us from this progression of full revelation and
encounter has been removed.

The Holy Spirit opened my eyes to this understanding to remove what has limited me, and all of His sons and daughters. As I read the rest of the sentence in 1 Corinthians 13:9-10, the veil I believed remained was removed from my eyes. The imperfect knowledge of who He is, that was in part, disappeared. Now I position myself differently when receiving from Him. You and I can see and hear Him openly. We are progressively coming into completion from glory to glory, coming into full maturity and the knowledge of the Son of God.

So Christ himself gave the apostles, the prophets, the evangelists, the pastors and teachers, **to equip his people** for works of service, so that the body of Christ may be built up until we all reach unity in the faith and **in the knowledge of the Son of God and become mature, attaining to the whole measure of the fullness of Christ.**

(Eph. 4:11–13, NIV)

For completion to come about, the fivefold must be operating in such a way that the whole body is fully equipped, that we become mature, attaining the whole measure of the fullness of Christ. Completion is coming, and for completion to come about, everything we know about Him and ourselves in part must disappear! We are coming into completion, seeing Him for who He truly is and who we truly are from glory to glory. We will perfectly love one another because love has been perfected in us as we receive it straight from the source.

When I was a child, I talked like a child, I thought like a child, I reasoned like a child. When I became a man, I put the ways of childhood behind me. For now we see only a reflection as in a mirror; *then we shall see face-to-face. Now I know in part; then I shall know fully, even as I am fully known.*

(1 Cor. 13:11–12, NIV)

Now that we can see who the Father truly is, the second revelation that comes into focus is who He reveals us to be. As we see Him for who He truly is, He reveals who we are. He has complete knowledge of us; He created us. As we behold Him, He reveals who we are. He empowers us and reveals to us His thoughts and His truth of who we truly are. From that place we are transformed into the very image He has created us to be from the beginning of time. As we see Him in His fullness, we see ourselves in our fullness—"Now I know in part; then I shall know fully even as I am fully known."

As you encounter Him, imperfect knowledge about yourself also vanishes. We will no longer talk and reason like a child. We can put childish behaviors and insecurities behind us because we have seen ourselves for who we truly are. The childish things were a by-product of only knowing Him and ourselves in part. As you encounter Him, you will see and operate fully in the gifts, talents, and what He has invested in you and dreamed you to be from the beginning.

For completion to come about, the whole body needs to operate in this revelation. As I come to Him and encounter Him face-to-face—seeing Him for who He truly is and being transformed into the very image He dreamed me to be—I display Him and myself entirely. As I do that, it launches others into this same revelation. On and on it goes like a domino effect. Imagine the fivefold operated in this revelation as they equip His sons and daughters, "Until we all reach unity in the faith and in the knowledge of the Son of God and become mature, attaining to the whole measure of the fullness of Christ" (Eph. 4:13, NIV). This is when completion comes about: when we've been perfected in the knowledge of God, of Jesus, and of ourselves. What we've known and seen in part, the imperfection of the knowledge, shall be removed.

Isn't this what we are after as the five-fold, to give ourselves to equip His sons and daughters fully? If we withhold nothing from each other—just as He withheld nothing from us—then we will be a mature body. Greater encounters of who He is await us as His whole body is being launched into the fullness of who He is and who they are. This is our mandate, as a body of Christ, to go after with all our heart!

What will that look like? We will no longer need intervention. There will be no more need of someone teaching us, interpreting for us, hearing for us; everything will be open and clear. We will no longer need assistance. We will fully know God and be fully known, operating in the fullness of who He created us to be.

If we have no need for intervention or to have others hearing God on our behalves, what will remain? After everything passes away, the only thing that will remain is love. We all will be perfected in love for the Father and for each other, perfected into the revelation and experience of oneness with the Father (Eph. 3:18–19). This is His dream and vision for us as sons and daughters: that each one of us comes to completeness, experiencing the closest connection with Him possible. This is our glorious hour and mandate.

Recognizing His Voice
Since we have complete access to the Father, why does it seem so hard to hear His voice? Good question, I'm glad you asked. So often the Father is speaking; however, we have not yet learned to recognize His voice. As Huub and I lead prophetic schools, we often

see people start to recognize that hearing God's voice is much easier than they originally thought. People often doubt that they hear His voice; all the while they've been hearing His voice but simply didn't recognize it. It is so beautiful to see their eyes light up when they experience the ease of hearing their Father. We will often ask them to write down something they think the Father is saying. They will oblige, even though they don't think what they wrote down is from the Father. More often than not, someone will prophesy over them confirming what they just wrote down.

We all have a unique way we communicate with the Father. If we think it has to be or look a certain way, we will miss what He is saying. It is so vital that we become aware of the ways He speaks to us so that we don't buy into the lie that He isn't speaking. His sheep, His sons and daughters, hear His voice. Why would He make it hard for us? It comes easier than we think. Hearing Him should be as simple as breathing.

Sometimes He speaks straight to your spirit. Maybe you hear just one word or sentence, and it goes straight to your spirit so that if you were to articulate what you experienced you would have a full story of the revelation of what just happened in your heart and spirit. For me, I hear Him say, "I'm taking all the pain away." Then I'll see flashes of memories where I experienced pain in relationships, disappointments and the pain I experienced. As they flash before me, I experience the pain that came with it leaving as He fills me with peace, comfort, and hope for the future.

Sometimes He will highlight something in the room, a person, or something they are wearing. Your eye falls upon something continually. In these times He wants to get your attention and speak to you about it. Ask Him questions to see what He wants to say regarding it. He wants to have a conversation with you.

This information can come so easily and subtly it could be dismissed. He wants to speak to you and share His thoughts He has about you. For example, something catches your eye—a sunrise, a mountain, a peaceful meadow, or a dad pick up their child, lifting them up high and smiling with great joy and delight. As this takes place, something happens inside of you. You might experience a sudden knowledge deep inside your heart that your heavenly Father looks upon you with the same great joy and delight. He gives you the full revelation of what He is saying without any need for words. It is His way of communicating with us spirit-to-spirit, heart-to-heart.

Some people see. They see pictures, words, or numbers in their mind's eye. The pictures can sometimes play out like a scene in a movie. Other times, they can be talking to someone and see images flash in their mind. They can seem like fleeting thoughts. Once while I was talking to someone, I saw the word "Ann" in my mind, so I asked them, "Do you have a coworker named Ann? Or a coworker whose name starts with A?" They responded that they did, so I continued sharing what I saw. "Do they have brown hair to their shoulders?" Once I had confirmed with them that who I saw was their coworker, I shared what I felt the Father was saying. In this case, I knew that He was using this person to impact Ann's life. And it all started with a word that flashed in my mind.

That may seem profound; however, it came naturally to me. It was so easy I could have dismissed it. That is why I tested it out with that person. If I were wrong about the name "Ann," I wouldn't have gone any further. However, because I was right, I leaned in to the Father's heart to learn why He was giving me that information. It was for a purpose. I fall in love with who He is every time I hear His voice for someone else in this way.

Hearing Him is a continual encounter we can enjoy with Him. Sometimes He speaks with an audible voice, and other times hearing His voice is so simple, it sounds like our own thoughts. When He speaks to me this way, it is usually confirmed in my spirit. Deep in my stomach I feel a warmth as the Holy Spirit burns within me. I will have a thought and share it, and I will keep going and lean into the Father to guide my conversation, being led by the Holy Spirit. When I talk to people, sometimes I follow that burning sensation in my belly to know that what I am speaking and hearing comes from the Father.

This happens in normal conversations, where sometimes the other person doesn't even know I am prophesying. However, when I share what the Father is saying, it goes straight to their heart and they are deeply moved. When they ask where I got all the wisdom and insight, it is my great pleasure to tell them it is from Jesus.

If I speak past that burning, I sense it in my spirit. I know I have to search for where He is speaking next. Or else I stop, wait, and listen again. We can easily do this in the midst of a conversation or even as we share in a meeting. It is as simple as following the Holy Spirit and letting His wisdom and revelation flow as we speak. Discovering the way the Father speaks to you could be challenging at first. However, the more you practice hearing His voice, the quicker you recognize it and the more confident you'll become.

Continual Connection
Hearing our Father's voice should be as simple as breathing, a continual two-way conversation. That is what it means to pray continually (1 Thess. 5:17). To practice this, you can shift your thoughts from thinking to yourself to thinking to God. Watch Him surprise you as He releases wisdom and solutions as you go about your day. It is not only about carving out time in your agenda to be with Him

by yourself at home, but communicating with Him wherever you go. In all your ways acknowledge He is there, and He will communicate back and direct your path (Prov. 3:6). You are connected to Him continually.

He is with you everywhere you go. If you asked Him into your life, He has made His home, His dwelling place in you. Since He lives inside of you, I would suggest that you might need to become more aware of Him. We become aware of His presence and from that place recognize what He is saying and doing in every situation.

It is important that we realize that He is speaking continually. We will then position ourselves to listen and receive instead of petitioning and striving. When you receive, hear, sense, or see something, it is important that you don't push it aside, denying that it came from the Father because of how easily it came to you. Why would He make it hard for us to hear Him? It should be normal for us to hear and recognize His voice. Let Him awe you as He unfolds who He is and who you are, details of people and places, letting you see who you will connect with before you meet them. Recognizing His voice takes practice, continually posturing ourselves from a place of persistent connection and relationship with Him.

At first, it can feel like you don't recognize He is speaking, but He is still speaking. He speaks in one way and another way and then in dreams (Job 33:14). A couple of reasons why we don't hear His voice is when we believe we don't hear Him or when He reveals something to us and we dismiss it without testing it out.

I once met someone who didn't believe God could speak to them through dreams. However, they had a dream about where

Huub and I would live. In the dream they saw us moving to the city where they worked. They didn't realize, however, that the dream was from God. Huub and I were supposed to move to that city, and we live there to this day! His sheep, His sons, and daughters, hear His voice. Whether you are aware of it or not, He is speaking.

If we think His voice must look or sound a certain way, we'll miss it. If we believe that we can only pray in one location, we've missed out on a continual walk, a daily adventure with the Father. If we believe that His voice only sounds like a deep, audible voice, we'll miss it all the times He spoke in a still, quiet voice. I've encountered many people who have become disappointed because they have an idea of how God's voice should sound. Meanwhile they've been hearing Him the whole time. Do you have any ideas of the way you think it should sound? What are they? Think about the times when you know you heard His voice. Learn the language you have with the Father. Practice it until it is sharp and accurate.

Trust
As you spend time with Him, you learn the way He speaks and you build trust with Him. Jesus calls Himself the Good Shepherd and we are His sheep. He continually speaks to us, calls us by name, draws us out, and we learn to trust Him. Just as sheep trust a shepherd, we build a thankful trust in Him as He consistently cares for us, brings us home, feeds us, and leads us to security.

Have you ever been to a sheepfold? I have been to a sheepfold in the Netherlands, and I couldn't tell the sheep apart. They all looked the same. For a shepherd to know all of his sheep by name, he must spend time learning the unique characteristics of each one. Yet, John 10 depicts Jesus as the Good Shepherd, saying that he calls them by name, "and his sheep follow him because they **know his voice**" (John 10:4).

The Father has distinct knowledge of each of us. He created us, and He knows us. Just as sheep learn to trust the shepherd and follow his voice, even into unknown territory, we can follow His voice and direction in our life, knowing that we can trust Him. We step out in trust, knowing He always has our best interest in mind. Even through the difficulty or pain we may have endured, He has always proven Himself faithful and been with us.

As we remember all of those past times of faithfulness, trust is built. With each step we grow in great confidence and boldness of who He is for us. After experiencing who He has been for me in the past, I become confident and bold in my trust in Him as He leads me. When He says go, as uncomfortable as it may be, I step out with confident trust saying, "Yes, I'll go if you're going. If I have you I can do anything!"

John 10:5 says, "But they will never follow a stranger; in fact, they will run away from him because they do not recognize a stranger's voice." The sheep simply will not follow a voice that is not from the shepherd. In fact, it is easy for them to discern the voice of a stranger, because it is foreign and unfamiliar; it is strange. Now that we recognize His voice and spend time with Him, it is easy to discern His voice among the rest. And we can be confident in following His voice because we recognize the Good Shepherd, His voice, character, and sound and the impact it has as we receive it.

Jesus, the Good Shepherd, lived His life as an example for us to follow. He did only what He saw the Father doing. He saw the Father in every move He made. He was aware of the Father every moment, and continually talked with Him. In like manner, we can become even more conscious of the Father and what He is doing in every step we take. We get to live in a continual encounter with Him as we learn to trust His voice.

Practice

So many people go from conference to conference, from school to school, and read book after book to learn how to hear God's voice. That is great, however, after a while, it will all come down to this: practice! You need to practice hearing His voice. What I mean by this is learning how to talk to the Father. Ask Him questions. When He speaks, write it down. Test what you heard by asking those around you for confirmation. By doing these things, you will begin to recognize His voice. If you miss it, that's not a problem. You just learned. That is part of the training process.

An excellent way to practice hearing His voice is to remember what it sounded like the last time you heard Him speak. Another way is to remember what it felt like when you last sensed His presence. Revisit the times in which you knew for sure that He spoke or that you encountered Him. What did it sound like, what did it feel like, what did it look like? Let it replay over and over, and you will start to recognize His voice.

You have your own language with Him, in the way He communicates with you. The way He speaks to you is unique because you were created with such uniqueness, and He speaks in the very way you will understand. Some people's language is through creative art, poetry, writing, journaling, gardening, going for a walk, soaking, taking a shower, singing, and the list goes on and on. Think of something you enjoy doing, and it is very possible that the Father uniquely created you this way and it's your language with Him. Enjoy discovering your language with Him.

Don't compare the way the Father speaks to you to the way He speaks to someone else. I invited a group woman over to prepare prophetic creative art to instill identity in a group of young adults. One of the ladies who were preparing their prophetic art seemed like she was having a difficult time. All the other ladies were thriving with creative prophetic ideas and were so excited. My friend, who was not enjoying the same experience, is really prophetic, so I thought, *of course, this is not her language.* I stood by my dear friend and said, "Why don't you sing a prophetic song instead?" This simply wasn't her language in the prophetic realm. She could create prophetic art; however, it would be more work for her. Her language with the Father is singing. And she released a beautiful prophetic song for one of the young ladies.

Wouldn't it be such a bummer if she compared her language with that of the others, thinking that she didn't hear God's voice or perhaps thinking that she wasn't as spiritual at that moment? She is really prophetic and can hear God's voice well. This just wasn't the language she spoke with the Father. Take some time to explore what your language is, how He speaks with you. Practice and become confident in it.

You can also practice recognizing His voice by testing prophetic words you receive yourself or from others. Test it to see if it builds you up, encourages you, or comforts you. Did the word bring you closer to the Father, or do you feel far away? If you feel condemned, hopeless, or far away, this did not come from the Father. Even in His correction He gives us grace that empowers us to overcome. We will never feel hopeless. It is His loving kindness that leads us to repentance. When He speaks there is a solution and empowering grace released that causes us to overcome anything.

Sometimes when He shows us pictures or images, we may dismiss them because it seems like a fleeting thought or image. Right before I go to bed or right when I wake up in the morning, I often see images or scenes in my mind's eye. It would be easy for me to dismiss it because it came so easy and seems like a thought. However, when we are aware that the Father wants to show us something, we can test what we see. Sometimes when I see these images, I describe them to my husband and ask if they mean anything to him. Often he will tell me that what I am seeing just happened at his work, or it will relate to something he recently encountered. Because I was willing to step out and test what I felt the Father was saying, we are able to pray together for the people or situations that were revealed.

One morning, while my husband was in a church service ministering, I was at home still sleeping. Right before I woke up, I saw this person speaking negative things over my husband, things that went against who my husband is. I knew exactly what this person looked like in detail. In my dream I was there watching all this play out, and I declared that the words that were spoken over Huub would fall to the ground and not bear fruit.

I could have just shrugged this off and forgotten about it, but I chose to test this, to see if something had happened during the service. So later, I asked Huub, "Love, did you meet a person today that looked like this?" I described what they looked like. "Yes," he said. Then I asked if that person had spoken something negative. My husband had encountered exactly what I saw in my dream or vision. The Father was speaking! He cared so much about Huub at that moment that He let me see it. And the words that came against my husband became void. Seeing from the Father's perspective, we were moved by compassion for the individual who spoke against Huub, understanding that they were in a difficult situation. We took time together to pray for that person. I wouldn't have fully known it was God speaking to me if I hadn't believed that God spoke to me in my sleep, and if I hadn't tested it out and spent time practicing and learning His voice.

Adventures with God

When I was learning who the Father is and learning how He speaks to me, I would talk to Him everywhere I went. I called this my adventures with God. Being a Christian was never meant to be boring, but rather an exciting adventure. In my adventures with God, I would ask the Father questions and take risks by stepping out with what I was hearing Him say or asking me to do. No one taught me what a word of knowledge was. I was simply testing what I heard the Father say. At that time, I worked for a firm, and I would experiment with God at work.

One day I asked someone I worked with, "Do you play the saxophone?" He looked at me shocked and said, "Yes! Why?"

At that time, I actually didn't know what else to say; I hadn't gotten that far yet. I didn't know what to do once I tested the word to see if it were true. I had already shared everything I had heard. I waited to hear what the Father would say to me next. The first thing that felt right to say was, "That's good, maybe you should keep playing it." That seemed like a good enough answer for him. I was amazed.

Another time, a UPS driver came to drop off a package. I heard the Father say, "Give him a bottle of water." I struggled with it for a while. It seemed awkward. But I did it anyway. "Would you like some water?" I asked. He was shocked, and his response was "What church do you go to?"

I was also shocked at his response. I told him I felt like Jesus wanted him to have water, and I wasn't doing that to have him come to church. But I told him because he asked. The more I went on adventures and took risks, the more hearing Him and receiving things for people became easier and the more confident I grew when hearing His voice.

I loved the adventure God and I were on together. I couldn't wait to see what would happen next! One day I went to the mall, and He told me there was a pregnant woman, giving me a description of what she looked like. He also told me not to be shocked if I knew her. As I went to the store He told me to go to, I found someone I knew. I didn't know she had just got a job there, and I also didn't know she was pregnant.

I told her that I came there just for her; that the Father led me straight to her to encourage her. She was overwhelmed to tears with her encounter with Him. He is so much better than we think. Why would He send me to her? He saw her in the situation she was in and wanted to love her and encourage her where she was. He knows every detail about each person and desires for them to know Him for who He is and to know that He sees and loves them.

As we go on adventures with Him we learn how to hear His voice and operate in the gifts of the spirit. We can hear so much teaching; however, the learning is in the doing. That is how we discover how we uniquely operate with the Father, something that can only be taught by the Father and the Holy Spirit. Have fun—go on an adventure!

Words of Knowledge
The word of knowledge is when God reveals details of a person's life that you could have never known. There is a reason why the word of knowledge is given. It isn't only to tell that person something they already know about themselves—that wouldn't be beneficial

at all. The word is given **to bring a solution**. Its purpose is to bring healing, to provide a solution that empowers that person out of that situation. The word of knowledge also allows someone to experience that they are seen and known by God.

If I have a word of knowledge, I won't speak it out until I receive the solution. For example, say I received a word that an individual's father physically abused the individual. I wouldn't tell the person that word of knowledge. What would that profit them? They already know that. Instead, I would wait for the solution. After receiving the solution, I would release the word of knowledge to encourage and edify that person.

I have seen many people hurt when the word of knowledge is misused. Sometimes the information God reveals, if shared incorrectly, can leave a person feeling naked and exposed. However, if we wait for a solution, we will bring and experience an even greater encounter. Going back to my previous example, it could look like this: "Is it true that your father abused you when you were young? I want to tell you that your heavenly Father is not that way at all. He isn't angry with you. He is not waiting to punish you. He came to share this with me so that you can experience Him and know Him for who He truly is. And know how He sees you. He believes in you…"

Whatever I may hear and experience I will share. What a beautiful gift He has given us as we operate out of love, that it will truly be used to edify, comfort, and strengthen the body.

Interpreting Revelation

In learning to understand and interpret visions, dreams, prophetic words, and pictures, I found answers in the book of Zechariah. He has been a great example for me. If you read how Zechariah receives revelation and interpretation of what the Lord shows him, you will notice that he asks questions. We might want to understand things immediately; however, when we wait to receive understanding, we get the revelation that comes from Him instead of our own interpretation. He never gave us a gift to operate in apart from Him. His interpretation is worth the wait, however long it may take.

When He shows me a picture, I will sometimes immediately have the interpretation. I personally feel a burning sensation in my belly to confirm that what I perceive is accurate. It is like my spirit within me burns or bubbles up. It is like I'm watching a movie before my eyes. When I don't understand the scene, it will stop playing. I will ponder and consider what it can mean. I think up all of these good spiritual ideas of the meanings of what I've been taught. However, it just won't give me that confirming "Ah-ha!" that makes sense. So the movie stops playing until I get the correct interpretation.

The most brilliant thing I can do in these moments is to be like Zechariah, who says, "I don't know."

Then the angel who talked with me returned and woke me up, like someone awakened from sleep. He asked me, "What do you see?"

I answered, "I see a solid gold lampstand with a bowl at the top and seven lamps on it, with seven channels to the lamps. Also there are two olive trees by it, one on the right of the bowl and the other on its left."

I asked the angel who talked with me, **"What are these, my lord?"**

He answered, "Do you not know what these are?"

"No, my lord," I replied.

So he said to me, "This is the word of the Lord to Zerubbabel: 'Not by might nor by power, but by my Spirit,' says the Lord Almighty."

(Zech. 4:1–6, NIV)

Zechariah was brilliant. He didn't assume he knew what things were or what they meant. He certainly didn't use his own idea or interpretation, but he continued to ask for understanding. Even when he was asked, "Do you not know what these are?" he was brilliant and said, "No." He then received the correct interpretation of what he was being shown. He also engaged in conversation.

Then I looked up, and there before me was a man with a measuring line in his hand. I asked, "Where are you going?" He answered me, "To measure Jerusalem, to find out how wide and how long it is."

(Zech. 2:1–2, NIV)

We can receive so much more when we engage with what we are being shown. Ask questions. We receive more revelation by engaging. When I receive a picture or vision I don't assume what it is. I ask, "Father, I have no idea. What does this mean?" I expectantly wait and wait until He reveals to me what the true interpretation is. It can be a very uncomfortable place to be as I sit and wait because I would like to know the interpretation immediately. Another thing that makes it uncomfortable is that it makes no sense to me. However, every time the waiting is worth it. This is the beauty of it; I can know without a shadow of a doubt that He gave the revelation to me because there is no way I could have come up with it on my own. I am amazed by Him. It was worth waiting for His interpretation and revelation.

The Prophetic is a Gift

As we operate in the prophetic realm, we become a walking gift. We are not "the gift" in a puffed up way. Rather, in both word and in demonstration, we bring gifts of edification, strength, and comfort. We become a visual display of who the Father is, and what He is doing. You are His eyes; You are His mouthpiece, His hands, and His feet. What an honor and privilege it is to be a living demonstration of the Father on this earth.

Living as a prophetic person, I often see myself as overflowing with gifts for other people. Anyone who gives a gift is bursting with a sense of joy and delight for the person and for what they are about to receive. I'm usually full of delight knowing the benefit the gift will bring that person. It is the same with prophecy; sensing and experiencing how the Father wants to give a gift, I become wrapped up with the demonstration and revelation of His heart in the way He wishes to give the gift. Inside the gift are the powerful words that build up, encourage, comfort, and strengthen. A couple of great purposes of the gift is for that person to experience that they are seen, and known by God and to launch them into their destiny as He reveals who they truly are and His dream over them from the beginning.

Have you ever experienced a prophetic word that didn't seem like a gift? Many people have come to me to help them process certain prophetic words they received. For one reason or another, the word didn't sit well with them, or they felt judged, condemned, ashamed, or even further away from God. This experience doesn't sound like a gift, and it certainly doesn't line up with what the prophetic is supposed to do. Prophecy should build you up, empower you, bring you close to the Father, and help you discover who you are and how He sees you. His loving kindness leads us to repentance (Rom. 2:4) and in His correction He gives words full of empowering grace to overcome anything.

When getting a gift for someone, have you ever given a gift you wouldn't want yourself? Who willfully gives a disgusting, horrible gift to another person? No one—unless it is some kind of joke. And even then it is horrible to receive such a gift. That should be a great indicator to whether or not you truly are giving a prophetic gift. In prophesying and praying, it can sometimes be difficult when you are standing before individuals who have hurt you in relationship, stolen from you, tried to divide, or sought to drag your name through the dirt. This is when it is important to not release anything in the spirit that you wouldn't want to receive yourself. In those moments I will pray in the spirit, talking with the Father in my mind. As I receive His heart for the person I'm ministering to, I'm able to prophesy life, unity, love, peace, restoration, and comfort. I will prophesy forth who they truly are and know them not after the flesh (2 Cor. 5:16).

Have you ever received a gift from someone and experienced a sense of being known by God? Those are great gifts! When we receive words that confirm exactly where we are in life, we feel seen and known by the Father. When He gives us direction for our lives, it confirms what we are doing or who we are. It propels us into the future!

Sometimes gifts or words can be a true gift but mixed in with people's interpretation of it. Have you ever received a word and thought, *Some of these words make sense; however, some parts are totally "off,"* or *I have no idea what I can do with this?* You can just let those words that don't make sense go and not receive them. When people come to me, discouraged by a prophetic word they received, I encourage them to pray that the words that were not from the Father would not produce fruit in their life. Receive what fits and discard or return the gifts that don't.

Sometimes a prophetic word just doesn't make sense. When that happens I put the word on the theoretical shelf. Maybe it is for another time. I have received words that were not for the season I was in. Instead of trying to make them happen, I trusted the Father that He would bring it to pass every word that was from Him at the right time. I waited until I had a direction or leading or when I saw I could actually use that gift or word.

Time will tell if a prophetic word was from the Father or not. Occasionally someone will try to convince others that their words are prophetic—as if they have to convince the recipient that what they are getting is truly a gift—using phrases such as, "This is a word; I feel it so strongly," or, "I am never wrong," and "You should do whatever you can to make it happen." I take these words with extra caution. If someone does this, it doesn't seem like they are presenting a gift at all.

We are to follow the way of love, focusing on the recipient of the gift and not on trying to prove accuracy or be right. In a situation where someone doesn't understand a prophetic word I gave, I would rather ask the Father if He would confirm it. I would rather say I'm sorry and end up being right and have the word come to pass than try to convince the person that I heard from God. The gift of prophecy is not about us; it is about the other person and their heart connection with the Father.

If you prophesy, you stand in a powerful place. In the measure and capacity that we give prophetic words, we also need to take responsibility for those words. I will protect another person's relationship with the Father far more than proving that I am right. I have experienced many people hurt, where they went back to someone who gave them a prophetic word that didn't come to pass. They leave the conversation saddened because that person refuses to take responsibility for it, and the recipient is left with deep sadness over something they had believed and hoped for not coming to pass, leaving them with an empty promise and many questions.

Seeing this take place over and over in so many places in the body of Christ, I have purposed in my heart to see the prophetic restored to what it really is supposed to be: a gift to the receiver. In the case above, it is important that the person giving the prophetic word take responsibility for the word given, protecting the recipient's relationship and connection with the Father and restoring the recipient to the Father when he or she is disappointed.

We need to mature in receiving feedback. If you missed what God was saying, learn from it. Sometimes the interpretation gets lost in translation. I live in the Netherlands, and I know what it is to be misinterpreted or misunderstood because I come from a completely different culture. Sometimes we simply misinterpret what God is saying, or we add our interpretation to what He showed us instead of waiting to hear what He says. Other times we keep talking, adding more to what He said. This doesn't mean that we don't hear His voice at all. It means that we missed the interpretation. And we can mature by taking responsibility for our words.

Don't let missing the interpretation keep you from continuing to practice your prophetic gift. Don't let the enemy come in and beat you down. Let it go, forgive yourself, and follow the way of love even for yourself. Go back and replay the revelation again. Find out where it was that you may have added to His words or where you may have felt His spirit lift off. Whatever it may be, invite the Father to show you what He wanted to do. This will only make you stronger and more accurate in your prophetic gifting. You hear His voice. Keep going!

I have seen people experience great encounters through the powerful, beautiful gift that is the prophetic. I have also seen people devastated by its misuse. If we follow the way of love and take our eyes off ourselves, then the prophetic word remains a gift as it was intended to be. It is ok if we miss it. Take responsibility for what was said and pray love into the situation. Follow the way of love. Love never fails.

Transformed by Prophetic Words
Have you received a prophetic word? Do you remember it? What did you do with it? Prophetic words are meant to change us into our original design. What He says about us should define us and call us back to who we truly are, to the dream He had over us from the beginning. When the Spirit of the Lord came on Saul and he prophesied with the Prophets, he was changed into a different person (1 Sam. 10:5–7). Something happened to Saul as he came under the anointing of the prophetic. He had a life-changing encounter. When we encounter His word, it changes us; it transforms us from glory to glory.

To be made new in the attitude of your minds; and to put on the new self, created to be like God in true righteousness and holiness.

(Eph. 4:23–24, NIV)

When hearing His word of truth about you, it is important that we record, remember, and meditate on the words He has spoken to us. In that way we renew our minds to truth and put on our new self. My husband and I record all the words that we receive that speak about our identity. His powerful Word transforms our lives.

> From now on, therefore, we regard no one according to the flesh...Therefore, if anyone is in Christ, he is a new creation.
>
> (2 Cor. 5:16a and 17a, ESV)

The prophetic word changes our lens; it changes the way we view people, situations, and ourselves. What does this look like practically? Surely our opinions and perspectives of other people will get in the way. But if we can lean into the Father and hear what He says about someone, we will open ourselves to seeing through this new lens.

I have shut my eyes and ears off from being distracted by what I think of someone while I minister prophetically. I close my eyes to who they are not, and I sink into His thoughts and how He sees them. Then, when He speaks, His heart fills me with compassion and truth about the person. He says to me, "Miranda, if you knew what this person went through you would have compassion." "Miranda, I am proud of this person and how far they have come." I am continually amazed with who He is, and who He is changes my view of others. As my heart softens, I am full of compassion; it is from that place that I hear and encourage.

In the same way, how He sees me changes what I believe about myself. When He tells me He believes in me, or that He is with me and will make me a success, it changes my view of each situation. I remind myself of what He has said, and it changes everything. It is only by His love and empowering word, His presence and face shining upon me, that I am empowered. Be empowered by His continual encouraging words. Write them down. Let them define who you truly are as you experience Him for who He truly is.

Activation: Receive Prophetic Words

Declare this over yourself: "I break off any lie I believe that spiritual gifts were for others and not for me. Today I choose to believe the truth that the gifts are for me. And I choose to follow the way of love and operate out of each gift from a place of love for the Father and for the people He shows me."

What are the gifts and talents He wants you to invest in so you can mature and have more influence?

1. Jesus, will You show me someone who I can encourage and how?

2. Father, who will You be for me in my dream life? What promises do You have for me?

3. Jesus, who will You be for my home, family, and/or marriage? What promises can I stand on?

4. Father, will You give me promises and encouraging words for my church?

5. Father, how do You see my city? Will You show me promises You have for my city?

Blessing and Impartation:
I pray that your eyes and ears be opened, that all of your senses are awakened in the spirit to become more aware of Jesus. I pray that any other voice that is not from Jesus will be foreign to you so that you will not be misled. Let hearing His voice for yourself and others be like breathing in all its simplicity. I bless you to go on adventures with the Father, to be wowed and in awe of Him. I bless you to have fun! See what you can do together!

CHAPTER 10

REVEALING THE FATHER

I am convinced that we are going to experience greater encounters of who the Father is by what He is doing. He is revealing Himself through prophetic words, encounters, dreams, visions, healings, and more. It is my hope that as you read this chapter, it launches you into even greater encounters with the Father—both for you and the people around you—seeing Him revealed for who He truly is.

For years, I would get irritated and jaded when people would share their visions, encounters, healings, and testimonies of things happening in their ministry. It was like I was hearing this loud noise, like a clanging cymbal or someone singing off key, and it would leave a loud ringing in my ears. I would cringe on the inside thinking to myself, *we are missing something*. And I was going to find out what that was.

As I continued to encounter this feeling, I would cry out to the Lord in my heart, *Something is not right; I am missing something! Let me reveal you as you really are. Reveal to me how to do it. Change me! Transform me into love.* When I heard people's testimonies, I was happy that they had an encounter or breakthrough, but something was off. *What is the clanging cymbal?* Then I realized that it is the sound we make when we do things, minister, or share encounters with any motive other than love.

We must ask ourselves, W*ho am I revealing when I minister or share an encounter? When people leave my presence, are they more impressed with me and my spirituality or with who the Father just revealed Himself to be?* When we forget to focus on who the Father is revealing Himself to be in our various experiences, we miss sharing and experiencing the greatest encounter of all—the love of our Father.

If I do not come to realize who God is revealing Himself to be when receiving or sharing prophetic words, visions, or dreams, my focus will be more on the colors, the brightness, and the hype of what is happening. When this happens, I do not reveal Him. Or perhaps more precisely, I do not reveal Him entirely or accurately.

After receiving a revelation, vision, dream, or word of knowledge, I ask questions. *Father, who are You revealing Yourself to be right now? Why would You share this information? Why would You give this dream or vision? Why would You tell me this before it happens?* I can tell you without hesitation that the answer has never been because I am so spiritual. The answer has always been, and will always be, because He loves so well, He sees us and knows every detail of our life, and He cares. That is why He reveals Himself to us.

The Magnifying Glass
Every dream, vision, prophetic word, healing, and revelation reveals a beautiful expression of who God is. That is my focus when testimonies are shared; I look to see if I can find Him. When I do, I bask in who He is as a part of His character is being revealed. He

is so much better than we know, and I want to reveal Him and look for Him in everything I see. I so desire to see Him revealed.

For example, I can have a vision or a dream that is highly detailed, and people may think, *Wow, Miranda is so spiritual. How does she know these things?* However, when we take the magnifying glass off the person sharing the testimony and focus instead on what He is doing and saying, then we will learn who God is through what He is doing.

Shift your magnifying glass onto God as I share the following vision. Let the details of the encounter be an encounter for you in your life and situation. Let God reveal Himself to you. One day as I was talking with the Father, He showed me a vision like a motion picture. I saw myself dancing on the sea with Jesus. We were dancing upon a great, roaring hurricane. The waves were crashing all around me, but I was not concerned: I had perfect peace as I danced with Jesus. He made the places where we danced upon firm and stable. I knew there was no way I would sink. I was completely captivated by Him and His love and peace, yet the storm continued around us.

Then, He took my hand and led me to a beautiful grassy meadow. I leaned back on Him as we sat down. I fit perfectly under his arm. I heard Him say, "And you will eat the good of the land." I soaked in the comfort of His arms as we ate the good of the land. I stayed there and remained with Him even though the sea was still roaring. I thought, *I have peace and the storm is raging, and I will eat the good of the land.*

As I came out of the beautiful vision, I began to get a sense that something was about to happen. It was like in the Bible when God says, "Fear not," at a moment when the people are about to freak out. I pondered this sensation for a while with the Father, but I didn't hear anything. Instead, I got up and went downstairs to tell my husband. I shared everything the Father showed me with my husband. We both pondered what it could mean.

A few hours later, the postman dropped a piece of mail in our door slot. This wasn't just any piece of mail, it was a blue envelope. Everyone in the Netherlands knows what a blue envelope means: the Dutch IRS. I opened the piece of mail reluctantly. We were being audited from 2009 to 2013. As the process went on, it turned out that we owed over 10,000 euro, plus interest! We were given invoices and had to make the payments on time, or we would have to pay even more interest. We had no clue this was going to happen. I have an accountant in America and thought everything was going just fine. We did what we thought we were supposed to do. Apparently it hadn't been correct, and now we had to pay over 10,000 euro. However, Huub and I were both amazed with the incredible peace we felt—a peace that would not let up despite the storm around us.

So why would God give me this vision? Who was He revealing Himself to be? I love to ask questions when receiving revelation from Him. If God were a distant God in heaven, why would He let me know this was going to happen? He would know it would all work out. He could have worked it out behind the scenes, sent some angels down, given me peace, made sure the money we needed came through; but why would He bother telling me it would be ok, showing me things before it happened to prepare my heart? He not only warned me, but He also showed me that He was going to provide for me and give me His perfect peace, and He did it in such a loving way. I am overwhelmed with who He is to us. He is a loving Father who provides everything His children need.

I am a person who can live off of nothing. I was once a student, and I ate macaroni and cheese and ramen noodles, so I knew I could do it again. But He said we would eat the good of the land. As far as I'm concerned, ramen and macaroni is most certainly not the good of the land. Steak is the good of the land! Fresh fruits and vegetables are the good of the land.

We did eat the good of the land. We ate so good, you would never know we were paying down such a large debt unless we told you. We had people over as we ate the good of the land together. We even had money to give to others. God really did provide for us. We were able to pay every cent on time and with ease. Money came to us. Huub even got an incredibly unexpected bonus with his work. It was amazing!

God provided so well for us; I am thankful I have Him. He cares about every detail in our life. He is there, He sees us, and He loves on us so well. Let who He revealed Himself to be in our lives minister to your heart. He will be the same for you in your situation. You can confidently look to Him in every situation in life, share the secrets of your heart with Him, and allow your thinking to become a conversation with Him as you go about your day. He will also share His secrets with you. He takes care of you and provides for you and desires to do even more for you as you invite Him. What a beautiful relationship!

As you experience an encounter with the Father yourself, let that encounter go deep by asking Him questions. When hearing testimonies, encounters, or visions in someone's personal life or personal ministry, remember to put the magnifying glass on God. Fall in love with who He is even more each time, and come into an encounter with a loving Father, knowing He is revealing one of His attributes and will do it again for you. He loves so well. Drink, delight, and think upon His love. Every revelation of His goodness is like a celebration feast set before you.

Revealing the Father through Dreams and Visions

Have you ever had a dream, revelation, or prophetic word for someone? Have you ever wondered why you received that word? Ponder that for a moment. Why would you receive that word of encouragement? I believe it is because God loves that person so much He wants to see them come into their fullness.

I have sometimes shared dreams I've received for other people. A lot of people are amazed and might forget to think about the One who gave the dream. I don't always share dreams I have for people; instead I intercede for them, unless I really feel that sharing the dream will provide a solution for them. I once had a dream where I saw someone I know being critical, negative, and hard on themselves. The Father wasn't angry with them, but I heard Him say, "This ends now." I decided to go to that person and share my dream with them. I asked them if it made any sense to them, and they went into detail about how they were struggling with self-criticism. Before they could say anything else, I said, "Isn't He such a loving Father who cares so much about you that He would give me a dream at night? The Father sees you, and this ends now!" How incredible to know that the Father cares about the details of our lives.

Another time I had a dream where I saw someone I knew weeping and deeply grieved, as though they had lost someone. However, their grief was caused by feeling alone. This person is usually very happy. In my dream I was encouraging and praying for them. When I woke up, I prayed for them and decided not to share the dream. Instead, I declared things over their life that I heard in the spirit. The next morning when I saw them, we stood side by side, laughing and enjoying life.

Unless I have a solution, wisdom, or revelation for someone in a dream, I don't share it. I usually find those dreams are meant for intercession. However, as much as I don't share dreams, as I stood beside them, I suddenly said, "Hey, I had a dream about you last night." I was shocked that I had said anything, and I couldn't think straight. This person was all ears, but I had nothing to say. I started talking with the Father, and I felt like He told me to just open my mouth. So I started talking, describing the dream. Then I sensed God's presence upon me as I shared with them the beauty of the Father's love—that He sees and knows exactly what they were going through. I shared how special it is that He sends someone a dream at night to encourage someone else. He cares about every detail in our lives. Tears poured down their face as they shared that they had never felt so seen and loved by the Father. This is why He gives dreams. He wants us to know and experience His love for us. He loves us enough to send me and you to reveal His heart and His passion. We might think these things are small and He doesn't see it or care. But He does.

Having a dream, vision, revelation, or an encouraging word can seem so spiritual. However, this is the way the Father communicates to us, and everyone should be experiencing Him communicating to him or her in this way. He uses these experiences and moments to lavish His love on us, to show us that He sees us, to let us know He is there. A good question to ask when having one of these types of encounters is, why? Why is He giving this revelation? Who is He revealing Himself to be? For whom is He revealing Himself? If we don't ask these questions or ponder reasons why we receive revelation, then we are missing out on a great encounter of who He is revealing Himself to be. When we hear His voice, we learn who He is.

Looking to Him

Many people get healed because they see a person operate in power, and they hear about their ministry and put their faith in that person. What if we had that same expectancy of faith because we have heard and seen who the Father is (Mark 10:52; Mark 5:34; Matt.15:28)? When we shift our focus from a person to our great and powerful God, we come into an even greater encounter of who He is. Imagine what God longs to do and show us as our eyes look not at man, but at the One who heals.

His kingdom is both at hand and nearby. What would happen if we knew the Father so well that we became convinced that He would meet us and heal us right now? As He reveals Himself to us, we will have a greater expectancy that He will meet us where we are at, because that is who He is. The idea that there is a great distance between Him and us is removed as we see and encounter Him for who He truly is.

As we learn to put our faith and trust in God and not the well-known person who can lay hands on us and pray for healing, we start to remove the "us versus them" mentality. I am certainly not saying that we shouldn't receive from people or receive impartation, which is biblical. However, God loves to use each person to encourage, heal, and lift up others, but when we focus too much on people who operate in power and are dynamic, we can spiritually disqualify ourselves and ultimately deactivate ourselves from functioning in gifts and power that are meant for everyone. The Holy Spirit lives in you. The same Spirit that raised Jesus from the dead is in you. Start activating yourself to walk with Him by healing the sick. Lay hands on yourself and others. Set your eyes on the giver of the gifts, and learn to earnestly desire not just the gifts, but also the most excellent way of operating in them, which is in love.

We are His Hands, Feet, Eyes, and Arms

My husband and I were leading a worship and prophetic evening, and in my mind, I saw myself go to someone and wrap my arms around that person. I knew the Father wanted to wrap His arms around her. So I went to that person, and as I wrapped my arms around her, pictures began flashing before my eyes of times this person was alone, different moments when they were crying out to God. As I watched and waited for the Father to speak, I heard Him say, "I have longed to hold her in my arms; I can't do it but you can." In His voice was such a deep longing that it gripped my heart. At once I realized we are His hands, His feet, and His arms extended to the world. I am a representation of Him to the people around me.

I shared with this individual what I heard the Father saying as I described each situation they were in, and I held them in my arms as I explained how the Father longed to hold them. I told them how He has been with them in each situation. He sees them and loves them. It was a beautiful moment.

I was overwhelmed with the honor of being God's arms to the people around me. He sends us to reveal who He is and what He is doing. He is doing so much; we only need to realize what He is doing so we can partner with Him. As I ministered to this person, they could see that they were hearing His voice all along and that He truly saw and loved them and that they were not alone. He is a loving Father. I love to be in that place where I get to experience who God is to others. I am in awe of Him.

God partners with us to display His glory. It is an honor and a delight to experience His loving heart. Being His arms that wrap around people and expressing who He is. People have said to me, "When I look into your eyes, I see the eyes of Jesus," or "When you wrap your arms around me, it is like being in the arms of Jesus, and I feel His love so tangible and thick." When I hear this, I become more aware of the Father operating through me. As a reminder to myself each morning, I say, "Father, I am your eyes, I am your hands, I am your arms to wrap people in, I am your feet." The more I become aware that I display the Father who lives in me, the more I see people changed by His love and presence. You can also become aware of God in you and position yourself like this in your life; see what happens!

Washing Away Judgment and Criticism
While at a retreat, I met a person who seemed a little rough around the edges when my husband and I were near them. They would get snappy and tell my husband that he needed to carry my things for me. My husband and I opted to be kind to them through some awkward moments. At one point, all the retreat attendees were sharing what we encountered during worship. This person said that they saw puppies and went on about a candy store. Not being able to identify with them, I pushed down any critical ideas with positive ones, reminding myself that while I couldn't relate, it is good the Father is restoring their childhood.

However, when I got in the car with my husband I started laughing, saying, "I saw puppies." Immediately, the Father said to me, "If you only knew what they have gone through and how far they have come, you would not be laughing." I was speechless. He said, "You are to go to them and encourage them." I said, "Father if I do it, it has to be real. It has to be true. It doesn't feel real at this moment." Telling Him this did not change a thing, so I asked,

"Please Father, make it authentic; make it not fake so that it can be real encouragement."

Later that day I ran into that person, and I wanted to walk straight past them. However, I decided to approach them and try encouraging them. So I started with some small talk. Then I said exactly what the Father said to me. I said, "Do you feel misunderstood by people?" They confirmed that they do feel misunderstood. I then told them that the Father is jealous over them, and He has their back. "You have come so far, and the Father is so proud of you," I shared. They broke into tears. I started telling them all the things He had just said to me, and I was moved with compassion as I saw them with God's eyes of love. After that, the rest of our time together at the retreat was so much nicer. It is so much more enjoyable to see people how the Father sees people, to lean into Him to hear what He has to say about their lives. Life is so much richer when it is free of judgment and criticism.

Prophetic Word to Europe
In 2005, I was given a prophetic word through a well-known prophetic network. At the time, I was receiving training from Encounters Network in Franklin, TN. One day they asked me to stay after class because they had a word for me. They gave me a word that I was called to Europe, that it was a mandate from God. They said there was a door that was opened to me—something to do with heritage—and I was to go there. They shared about all the things that would happen there when I went. I said, "I'm not called to Europe, I'm called to Africa." They said they didn't hear anything about Africa, and they encouraged me to wait on Africa and go to Europe. They continued sharing until the Holy Spirit gripped me, and I deeply groaned within my spirit. I didn't understand everything that was said, but since they recorded the word, I was able to listen to it later. When I got up to leave, I didn't know

what to do with the prophetic word, so I just set it aside and carried on with my life.

In January 2008, I was gearing up to go to Uganda with a friend of mine. However, during that time I met Huub and we were getting more serious. We have a wild and wonderful story of how we met. Around that time I felt like the Father said I was supposed to go meet his family. Huub is from the Netherlands. At the time, it didn't occur to me that this was the door for me into Europe. I didn't have a heart for Europe, so I hadn't put it all together. I made it clear to him that I wasn't going to live there, and I couldn't ask him to move to America to leave everything behind, but he did anyway. I waited on Africa, and I went to Europe to meet Huub's parents. All the while, I didn't realize that I was fulfilling the prophetic word.

After we got married in August 2008, Huub needed to leave the United States in order to get a visa. We needed to live in the Netherlands for six months as we processed papers. During this time, I started to encounter the people in our town in the Netherlands. When I would share about who the Father is and stories about Him in my life, they were so hungry and deeply moved that these things might also happen to them. It gripped me time and time again. I would go to bed thinking about them. I could sense the Father and the Holy Spirit yearning for them. One day I was working alone at my desk, and the Father said to me, "You are to live here." I immediately started weeping, "I know," I replied. Then the Spirit of the Lord came upon me strongly, and I sensed deeply the Spirit yearning and longing for the people.

The Father was revealing to me a part of His kind and gentle nature. He was not commanding me to go to Europe. I didn't know anything about Europe. I didn't have it in my heart to be there at all. However, He was showing me how by being there I would encounter the people and fall in love with them. It was as though He was inviting me there, as if He was saying, *You don't know yet how much you will love it. You don't know how much your heart and passion will be for the people here and how much you will thrive by living here.* And it is true, I have beautiful sleepless nights replaying wonderful moments of how our lives are being used to impact others and seeing people come alive.

Transformation by Revelation

> **Let the message about Christ, in all its richness, fill your lives.** Teach and counsel each other with all the wisdom he gives. Sing psalms and hymns and spiritual songs to God with thankful hearts. **And whatever you do or say, do it as a representative of the Lord Jesus**, giving thanks through him to God the Father.
>
> (Col. 3:16–17, NLT)

In other translations, it says, "Let the word of Christ dwell in you richly." Have you ever received great revelation and thought to yourself, *Oh, that will preach,* or, *that's a good word* and immediately wanted to share it in a church service or post it on Twitter or Facebook? In moments of revelation, I have had to shut off my desire to share what it is I am seeing or learning so I can let the message, in all of its richness, fill my life instead.

When we receive revelation, whether through the Bible or directly from God, we can be too quick to share it instead of letting it go deep and fill us with wisdom. Part of deeply encountering His word and being able to counsel and teach others is first understanding what He is saying to you and letting it have its full work in your life so that you become the living word in action. This allows us to live out of relationship with God and not ministry. How much more powerful is it to be a living demonstration than to simply have a good word to preach?

One day I was preparing for a meeting with a group of people about prophetic art. I am convinced that one of the best ways to positively change culture and the world is through the arts and entertainment. As I was preparing some questions about the book we were reading together, I was going through it like a wild woman. I had to be prepared for the meeting in a few hours. I heard the Father say, "Go slower; read it for yourself. Don't you think that I also want to show you some things through this book?" All at once I knew I am not exempt. The Father wants me to grow just as much as I want those around me to grow. I was deeply affected by how He cared about my growth just as much as He and I cared about the growth of others. You and your growth are just as important as the ones you are leading, and it is from that place of revelation and growth that you can truly be a living demonstration and the living word in action.

Activation: Greater Encounters with the Father

1. Ask the Father to remind you of times He showed up for you in your life. As moments flash before you, ask the following questions:

   Who were You revealing Yourself to be?

   Why did You say what You said when You knew everything would be ok?

2. Revisit encounters you've had with the Father, and ask Him to reveal why He showed you things. Ask Him questions to understand the different facets of who He is.

3. Practice asking who the Father is revealing Himself to be when giving encouraging prophetic words, when someone is being healed, or when His power is being manifested in some way.

4. Practice focusing on who the Father is revealing Himself to be when receiving or hearing prophetic words, visions, or dreams. Enjoy greater encounters of who He is.

CHAPTER 11

THE GREATEST IMPACT

Have you ever thought, *Why is it taking us so long to impact the whole world?* With so many churches and so many Christians, how is it possible that we haven't changed the world by now? What is causing us to go so slowly? This question is constantly on my mind. What is it that we are missing? The church is a great and glorious, edifying and equipping greenhouse. It is a loving family from which we are launched into every realm of influence. The church is not a building but His body, a family of His sons and daughters living in the reality of heaven on earth. We simply need to put this truth into practice. My hope is that this book and this chapter shine light on how to shut down anything that might cause us to go slower or lose momentum. Instead, I long to see the church step into its fullness so that we can have the greatest impact on this world.

When my husband and I speak anywhere or prepare for any meeting. I ask the Father what He and I can do that will have the greatest impact. I thoroughly enjoy asking that question all the time. I am constantly asking the Father for wisdom and revelation on how to bring about the most effective change. How can we have the greatest impact and also a lasting one? I want to leave something that lasts.

I come alive when I ask these questions. Pondering about how to leave a lasting impact causes me to dream over people's lives and over different places. I spend time with the Father asking Him, "If I were to do this, what will the outcome be?" I let the steps and ideas play out in my mind, dreaming about that outcome that will leave a lasting mark on people's lives. I make sure the dream aligns with the culture of heaven, and His heart then, when everything lines up, I GO FOR IT with all my heart.

In my dreaming, planning, and everything I do, my aim is to hit the mark of God's heart. Like an arrow being shot out, His heart is my target. My eye is fixed; my gaze is set to hit the mark of His heart (Phil. 3:14). My purpose is to make sure the ideas and dreams line up with His heart for the people or the place I am going to. I wait to receive His instructions, wisdom, and insight. As His plans become clear, everything else, those things surrounding me to distract me, tune out. All the other voices are silent. I will not be distracted. When everything lines up and is set, I release the arrow—the idea, dream, or plan in living action—with everything in me; I release it. I keep my eyes open and watch to see—*did I make it?*

Hitting the mark of His heart means to stay fine-tuned and focused on the impact that you want to have that lines up with His heart for the people you are influencing. We can easily become distracted by things that don't matter but look significant or seemingly important. Just a slight distraction here and there sets us off course. However, when all the other voices are tuned out— people's opinions or criticisms as you step out into your dream or something God has called you to do—you can focus on why you are doing what you are doing. Focus on His heart keeping your heart pure before Him. And when the plans, dreams all line up, then go for it!

In dreaming with a friend of mine who is a beautiful, pure-hearted worshipper, I asked, "Why don't you start a website?" I have been greatly affected by her music and think it is a bummer that I, as well as others, am unable to hear the songs again. My friend said, "Oh, people will just think, *here she goes promoting herself.*" I then asked, "Why do you do what you do? When you believe in what you do, then you will want to reach the most people you can."

When you are living for something greater than yourself, you'll become bold and confident and other people's opinions won't matter anymore. Your passion and what you are going after will be unstoppable. As a worship leader, for example, when you hit the number one worship song on the charts, it will be wonderful, but you won't feel the need to compete to keep your position at number one. You will have a higher goal, a reason for doing what you do, and that will be your focus.

I shared about this earlier in the book, but I want you to revisit this question: Why do you do what you do? If your goal is to be the best in your field or the CEO of a company, those are great goals. However, what will happen after you reach that goal? What will you live for? What is the true purpose of attaining that place? When we live for impacting the lives of others, our focus shifts from ourselves to how our success can help lead others to success. This is how to hit the mark of His heart in what you do. Your life will not only mark history but heaven.

Just like the victory you have when you shoot an arrow out and it hits the target square in the center, what a glorious sight and celebration to see the impact it has on people's lives when we hit the mark of God's heart. When my focus is to hit the mark of His heart in my life, I will never miss. He is my goal, and the effect He has is great and lasting when lives are changed by His great love. Each time, I sit back with the Father and drink in the beauty of who He is that is released. The sight of it is glorious, and I drink in those moments. It is what I live and thrive for. I bless you in all that you do to hit the mark of His heart, and when you do, enjoy the glorious celebration of the impact you and He will have on the world.

Making History
Around 2004, I had a vision that I was leaving a land. And as I was leaving this land, it turned into a mountaintop, like a cliff. As I took my first step off the cliff, there was a bridge that extended in the sky for me to walk across. I stepped onto the bridge and walked on it until I was away from the edge and could no longer see the cliff. When I got far enough from the land, the bridge began to crumble after me. There was no way for me to get back. I heard Him say, "I am removing from you any man-made structure." There was nothing left for me to walk on except my trust in Him, but I continued to walk forward as if I was walking on a bridge. My bridge of trust was invisible to the eye, but to me it was both steady and secure, so I kept walking in confidence.

After walking for a long time, there came a point where I couldn't walk any further. Something was blocking me from moving forward. I didn't know what to do. I realized the only way I could continue was if I were to lay my life down. So I knelt down and laid my body out as flat and as spread out as I could. Stretching myself as far as I could go and then my hands, as I reached out as far as I could, I was able to grasp with my fingertips the other side, reaching into the Promised Land. As I lay there, people began to come. I realized that my life laid down made a bridge for them to walk across into the Promised Land.

As the people came, I looked forward to seeing how many would come into the land. I thought there would be more than I could count. However, there weren't multitudes of people, and I asked the Father, "Where are the multitudes? Is this it? I am laying my life down for a few people?" Then I heard Him say, "They carry nations in their belly." That gave me a renewed perspective. I would be influencing people whose purpose would have an impact on nations! My life is laid down for the world-changers to come into their promise. What a different perspective! If you want to mark history, if you want to mark nations, begin by marking someone's life by helping them to thrive, setting them up for success, believing in them, giving everything possible to help them come into their fullness. That is how we enter into the promise of God over our lives.

Greatness in Leadership

Have you ever had your feet washed? I have and it is an incredibly humbling, yet beautiful, experience. When it was my turn to have my feet washed, I slowly and sheepishly placed my feet into the water, making some jokes to distract myself from the awkwardness I felt as I saw there were still pieces of sock stuck on my feet. I closed my eyes, thinking that if I couldn't see it, neither could they. I opened one eye, nope, still there; it is what it is. There was definitely sock floating in the water. Then the person washing my feet looked up and smiled as they lovingly cared for my feet—washing them, rubbing them and pouring oil over them, blessing me, praying, and prophesying. It was an expression of love that goes deep.

Now imagine that the person who is washing your feet is the president of the United States, the King or Queen of the Netherlands, or maybe Prince William or Kate Middleton, Princess Diana or your favorite actor or actress. What would that be like for you? Wouldn't it be a truly humbling experience? However, Jesus is the King of all kings, the Lord of lords, higher than any other president, royalty, or actor. He is God, and there is no one above Him.

Having the highest position in existence, Jesus displayed what a leader looked like when He washed the feet of His disciples (John 13:1–17). He showed us that He did not come to be served but to serve. At that time, the act of washing feet was an act that only servants did for their masters. Someone in a lower rank did this service to someone who had a higher rank. This was in their culture. Yet, the disciples sat and received from Jesus the act of a servant as Jesus displayed what it looked like to lead them.

What would that have been like had we been in the disciples' position? We might have walked through some dirty, muddy, and dung-filled places. Jesus would have seen it all, everything we walked through exposed on the bottom of our feet. He would have been able to smell it. But His love is safe, and His love washes it all away. We are meant to lead in this very same way. I doubt Jesus was shocked that the disciples had dirt on their feet. Maybe one had a bigger mess than another. Sometimes in our lives, we go down paths that are dirty, led astray by lies we once believed. Jesus washes it away with His truth. The way He sees us goes deep and transforms us.

We have this same opportunity to display such love and servanthood as leaders. The more people you are leading, the more people you are to love and serve in this same way. We are meant to be a safe place where people can expose their dirt and come get washed by the truth of who they are. It isn't about our title or position, but the love and impact we choose to have on the lives of the people we are serving.

Demonstrating this example of leadership doesn't mean you lose your leadership qualities and become a doormat for people. Leading in this way requires seeing people for who they are, not only what they do. It means having their best interest in mind, empowering them, and speaking God's truth over them. By leading as Jesus demonstrated, the people you are serving will feel safe as a culture of trust is developed and there is a heart-to-heart connection established.

We can display this in little actions to show that we see, recognize, and value each person we meet. I was at a leaders' meeting, and one of my heroes in the faith was there speaking. I was sitting behind him. So many people were coming up to him to talk with him, wanting to be seen with him. This is all going on, and he turns around and sees me. He puts his hand out to shake my hand, holds it firm, and looks straight into my eyes. As we talked, I felt seen and valued. It was like time stood still and the only people in the room were he and I. That made a lasting impression on me that I want to demonstrate to all the people around me. From that point, wherever I went, I would catch the eyes of people I walked past so they would experience the same sense of belonging—I see you, and I value you.

You Are Valuable

> The eye cannot say to the hand, "I don't need you!" And the head cannot say to the feet, "I don't need you!" On the contrary, **those parts of the body that seem to be weaker are indispensable, and the parts that we think are less honorable we treat with special honor.** And the parts that are unpresentable are treated with special modesty, **while our presentable parts need no special treatment.** But God has put the body together, giving greater honor to the parts

that lacked it, so that there should be no division in the body, but that its parts should have equal concern for each other.

(1 Cor. 12:21–25, NIV)

We are all members of a body where each member is vital and necessary for the full operation of the body. We have this idea of rank when it concerns people. However, the parts of the body that seem weaker are indispensable. That means they are vital. We have to shift our focus on what it means to be valuable. God sees us as a body working together beautifully, where each member is valuable and necessary. In fact, each member is just as important as the others.

Say we decided we didn't want to be a certain part of the body—the foot, for example—because its job is dirty or unglamorous. We would say to ourselves, "I don't belong to the body. I am not seen nor needed." If that is how we felt about the body, or our position within the body, we would be walking around handicapped. Imagine we were one body without an eye, leg, hand, or foot. Perhaps we are already living handicapped by our perception of ourselves and the body?

1 Corinthians says that the parts we think are less honorable we should treat with special honor. However, do we take the time to truly honor those who may not be in the spotlight? There are so many people around us who we don't see, but if we didn't have them, then we would miss them being there. I don't know who wants to be a garbage man, for example, but if we didn't have them, we would have a huge problem. The streets would become wastelands as people begin to throw their trash everywhere and anywhere. Every member of the body serves a great purpose and is worthy of honor and value, down to the smallest, most unseen

part. What's more important, however, than valuing each other for our role is valuing each other for who we are.

And the ones who are in the limelight, the presentable parts, should show no need of special treatment. What if we lived our lives in such a way that no matter what title we carry, we position ourselves to not require special treatment? Often we feel entitled to special treatment because of a specific position we carry. But rather than pursue the things we feel entitled to, what if we carried ourselves in a tangible, authentic, and real way? Honor is something that is given and not demanded.

Perhaps it is time we set a new model of leadership. As leaders, we set the tone for others to follow. So what is that tone? What culture do you want to see increase? It is important that we increase the culture where people are seen and honored, serving each other like Jesus did. I am convinced that when we model this, we will have a greater impact on people's lives. We will leave a lasting impression in the hearts of the people we encounter. And we will be showing the world who Jesus really is.

How to Cheat Death in Life
Have you ever been bothered when you read in the Bible that Moses was not able to cross into the Promised Land? When I read that, I am always deeply grieved. That must be one of the worst things to experience—having a vision for something and not be able to go into it yourself. Moses never got to go into the Promised Land, the very thing he was called to lead Israel into. He didn't get to taste its fruits. He gave of himself 100 percent so that Israel could enter in, and he got to see it, but wasn't able to enter it himself.

Then we have David; he wasn't able to build the temple for the Lord—his lifelong dream, vision, and passion. This dream was out of a heart's flow of passionate worship for the Father. However, he wasn't the one who was to build it. Has that ever messed you up when you read that? As I have read those passages, I have earnestly asked God, "Please, Father, let me taste what you've shown me; let me experience it. I don't want to live like they did."

Walt Disney is another example; he imagined and dreamed a fantasy world and never got to experience it for himself. Even Martin Luther King Jr. did not fully experience the full outcome of his dream. Before he died, he gave a speech in Memphis called "I've Been to the Mountaintop," in which he said:

Well, I don't know what will happen now. We've got some difficult days ahead. But it really doesn't matter with me now, because I've been to the mountaintop. And I don't mind. Like anybody, I would like to live a long life; longevity has its place. But I'm not concerned about that now. I just want to do God's will. And He's allowed me to go up to the mountain. And I've looked over. And I've seen the Promised Land. I may not get there with you. But I want you to know tonight, that we, as a people, will get to the Promised Land. So I'm happy, tonight. I'm not worried about anything. I'm not fearing any man. Mine eyes have seen the glory of the coming of the Lord.

The day after this speech, Martin Luther King Jr. was assassinated. He didn't get to experience the freedom we have today. However, his life shifted culture and marked history. Each of the leaders mentioned above were living for something beyond themselves. They had a vision they lived from continually. We can also live from a place where we are experiencing our vision, setting it before our eyes and letting it play out again and again as it is our reason for where we are going and why we are doing what we do.

David's passion was to build a house for God's Presence—the Ark of the Covenant to rest in. Even when he learned that he could not be the one to build the temple, David set his kingdom up for success by putting Solomon in his place. He did not withhold anything from him, but gave everything in his power in order to set Solomon up for success. David lived to have the greatest impact he could in his lifetime and beyond by leaving everything he had as an inheritance for his son and kingdom.

> King David rose to his feet and said: "Listen to me, my fellow Israelites, my people. **I had it in my heart to build a house as a place of rest for the ark of the covenant of the Lord, for the footstool of our God, and I made plans to build it.** But God said to me, 'You are not to build a house for my Name, because you are a warrior and have shed blood'...So now I charge you in the sight of all Israel and of the assembly of the Lord, and in the hearing of our God: Be careful to follow all the commands of the Lord your God, **that you may possess this good land and pass it on as an inheritance to your descendants forever."**

> (1 Chron. 28:2–4 and 8, NIV)

David instructed everyone to follow his example by possessing the land and passing it on as an inheritance to their descendants. Why? So that everything they worked for and gave themselves for would not be lost, but would be passed down from generation to generation. David instructed them to cheat death by letting their dreams and legacy live on after they were gone. He displayed what it looks like to be a great father and king and what it looks like to have a heart after God.

Then David gave his son Solomon the plans for the portico of the temple, its buildings, its storerooms, its upper parts, its inner rooms and the place of atonement. He gave him the plans of all that the Spirit had put in his mind for the courts of the temple of the Lord and all the surrounding rooms, for the treasuries of the temple of God and for the treasuries for the dedicated things…"All this," David said, "I have in writing as a result of the Lord's hand on me, and he enabled me to understand all the details of the plan."

(1 Chron. 28:11–12 and 19, NIV)

David didn't withhold anything! Besides his detailed plans for the temple, he also gave his personal treasures of gold and silver for the temple, even over and above everything he had already provided (1 Chron. 29:3). What was in David's heart when he did this? What was his focus? What was his understanding of success? For David, success was not determined by his position or what he owned. It was in loving God to the fullest and leaving a lasting impact for generations. What David lived for didn't die with him but lived on past his life. In this sense David cheated death.

David also said to Solomon his son, "Be strong and courageous, and do the work. Do not be afraid or discouraged, for the Lord God, my God, is with you. He will not fail you or forsake you until all the work for the service of the temple of the Lord is finished. The divisions of the priests and Levites are ready for all the work on the temple of God, and every willing person skilled in any craft will help you in all the work. The officials and all the people will obey your every command."

(1 Chron. 28:20–21, NIV)

I love how David encouraged Solomon and expressed who the Father would be for him. Because he would not be able to stand at his side and give him wisdom, David made sure everyone was prepared to help Solomon and receive him as king. What if your spiritual father, earthly father, leader, or employer set you up for success in this same way? How would this affect you? How would it affect the way you step into that position? David not only prepared Solomon and the people, but in doing so set up the entire kingdom for success.

> The people rejoiced at the willing response of their leaders, for they had given freely and wholeheartedly to the Lord. David the king also rejoiced greatly.

> (1 Chron. 29:9, NIV)

It is our turn to display this same example in the way we lead, living beyond our title or our own success and focusing our dreams on leaving behind a lasting impact. This type of leadership is contagious. The people followed David's example, giving willingly toward a dream—a place of worship that would survive long past their lifetime (1 Chron. 29:6). Solomon and the whole kingdom were set up for success, and they thrived. If we would follow his example, we would truly have a significant and lasting impact!

It is vital that we set people up for success in our lifetime as well as to serve and rule after us. Paul, the Apostle, raised his beloved spiritual son Timothy to lead, empowering and encouraging him, training him to step into a role of authority. The Bible is full of examples of what happens when we help bring others to a place of success and leadership, as well as what happens when we don't. What will you choose? Will you decide to let your legacy die with you, or will you cheat death by empowering the next generation to carry the dreams and purposes of the kingdom forward into their lifetime and beyond?

Empowerment

It takes a secure leader to see the gifts and talents in people, activate them in it, and give them room to grow. People will rise up and may be more powerful in their spiritual gifting than you are, or they may operate in a greater understanding of the spiritual realm. However, this is an indication that you are doing well! You are succeeding as a leader. Keep on going! Cheer them on and believe in them. Once people are given a place and a voice, and they are set up for success, they will thrive. And what a glorious sight it is. Your role as a father or mother is both significant and utterly necessary. We all have the opportunity to be the most excellent father and mother we can possibly be. Once we understand that and grab hold of it, we will truly have the greatest and most lasting impact.

> For though you might have ten thousand instructors in Christ, yet you do not have many fathers; for in Christ Jesus I have begotten you through the gospel.
>
> (1 Cor. 4:15, NKJV)

Paul wrote that the church had many tutors, many spiritual instructors but not many fathers. Paul's life became a demonstration of what fatherhood should look like. He lived to bring churches into their full maturity and in the love of Christ. He empowered Timothy to serve the church alongside him and to carry on after him. There is a great need in the world for more fathers and mothers who will empower and equip. This is what the world needs, and it is our role to demonstrate fatherhood and motherhood to the world.

As you step into this role, if any insecurity emerges—fear of not being needed or of losing your place—don't push it aside. Instead, expose it for the lie that it is. That is not who you are! Don't buy into the lie that could prevent you from impacting not only your generation but the generations to follow. Share the insecurity with the Father and ask Him what His truth is instead. It is important that you live an empowered life yourself. Lies about ourselves and about our success will only hold us back from being the greatest version of who we are.

He Promotes You

Now that we have shifted our focus to having an impact that out-lives us, we can be sure that our incredibly good Father will set us up for success. He promotes us. He goes before us like David went before Solomon, preparing people's hearts to receive us. He brings us into the place we need to be. I have seen it so many times in my life and the lives of others. One night at church, be-fore service began, a lady introduced herself to me. I heard the Father say, "She is a worshipper! Set her up to lead this weekend on Saturday." I was a little surprised because I didn't know any-thing about her. Later she and I had lunch together, and I asked her if she ever led worship. She said yes. We were both surprised because there is no way I could have known that. As we got to know each other more, I asked her if she would come and lead worship on Saturday morning. She was delighted about it and said she would love to!

The Father was revealing Himself as the one who promotes us. As we continued our lunch, I shared with the woman, "The Father promotes you. When you go places He will put it on people's hearts to make room for you." She burst into tears. I could feel the Father's heart for her as she shared how encouraged and refreshed she was from our conversation. He truly opens doors for us. The Father was revealing this truth to me as much as to her, and I learned to rest in that truth for my own life: He promotes me. He prepares the way for me, just as he prepared the way for this worship leader. She has had such an impact on our church family and has formed a lasting relationship with us. Rest in that truth, and lean on God who is promoting you and positioning you for success.

Activation: Changing the World around You

Every person is a leader. You are leading someone, whether you realize it or not. You come into contact with people and are an influencer. Everyone serves something or someone. Consider your job: What is God's purpose in having you working where you are, serving a company, church, group, and so on? Why do you do what you do? What is your goal in being there?

Our dreams and plans are like an arrow being shot out to hit the mark of God's heart. If we stay focused on His love, we won't miss that mark. If you need help knowing what dreams or plans you are meant to pursue, here are some great things to dream and ask Jesus about:

1. Dream about your community, your church, your city without limits, without any fear, without any financial limitations. What could it look like? What would you be doing? What is the first step you can make towards this dream?

2. How can I have the greatest impact as I serve those around me?

3. Jesus, Who are my spiritual fathers and mothers? People I need to be connected with that I can receive from? Reveal

to me those people You have placed around me to love me for me.

4. How can I "cheat death"? What are the most valuable things I am living for that I want to see live on after I'm gone?

CHAPTER 12

THE REVELATION OF
THE GLORY OF GOD

Full-time ministry is not limited to the church. Wherever you are, whatever you are doing, you are in full-time ministry. For too long the church has believed a lie that it is more spiritual to do ministry inside the church than anywhere else. So we quit our jobs and gave up our careers to go into full-time ministry. Unfortunately, if our eyes are focused only on the church, we lose our opportunity to shine in dark places.

Many great leaders in the Bible were not called to the church—Nehemiah, Daniel, Moses; consider their lives and influence. What would have happened if they had quit what they were doing in order to serve full-time in the temple or the synagogue? Worse yet, what wouldn't have happened?

Joseph was known for his excellence, often receiving wisdom and revelation from heaven and the interpretation of dreams. He had a gift, and he chose to operate in that gift everywhere he went. The Bible doesn't have any stories about how Joseph went to church and preached. He wasn't called to the church. Many great leaders in the Bible and present day are not called to the church but are meant to change the world by showing what it means to live a life connected with our heavenly Father—receiving wisdom and revelation for their particular realm of influence.

> Let your light shine before men in such a way that they may see your good works, and glorify your Father who is in heaven.
>
> (Matt. 5:16, NASB)

This verse doesn't encourage us to preach the word of God at men or argue theology with them. It tells us to let what is in us shine brightly before the people around us. It's really that simple. Let wisdom, love, joy, peace, and revelation shine bright in such a way that people can't help but acknowledge that God is with you, glorifying Him just like the scripture says.

Joseph did this very thing, even becoming a great influencer in prison. He even caused the prison to prosper (Gen. 39:20–23). Rather than trying to find a way out, he used his wisdom and gifting to create a better system. He did everything with excellence, and people recognized that God was with Joseph, and looking favorably on him and prospering everything he did. God showed Himself stronger and more powerful than other wise men and magicians in the land through Joseph. Everything he did presented the people with an opportunity to see God and glorify Him. This is how we are to position ourselves in the world.

Your Life Is Your Platform

Many people are waiting for a platform from which to speak or minister. However, your life is your platform. Your lifestyle speaks louder than any words or message ever could. Be yourself wherever you go instead of limiting yourself to a platform or a church. Be who you are wherever you are in the fullness of your beauty and shine.

After moving to the Netherlands, my husband and I were looking for a church to call our home. We were at a particular church, and during worship we both separately had an intense encounter where we heard the Father saying, "This is your home." We were exited and encouraged after sharing our encounters with each other. We served our church, fell in love with the people, and made relationships. It was and is home to us.

After a while, one of the pastors told us that we have had such a great impact and influence in people's lives and asked why we weren't on the leadership team. In fact, the leadership team had asked why we were not on the team. It had not occurred to us to even ask these questions because being part of the leadership wasn't our goal. Our goal is, and will always be, to express who we are everywhere we go. We live and thrive to impact lives, whether we are placed in leadership within the church or not.

Huub and I believe that we are called to edify, encourage, and train up His body, so we trust that the Father will set us up for success to do so. We want to see each and every believer experience the greatest impact possible in their respective area of influence, whether it is business, agriculture, arts, sciences, or the church! Unfortunately, many Christians believe it is more spiritual and holy to be doing something within the church, and we give up on incredible positions of influence in the world around us. However, it is time. It's time to train the church to hear His voice, His solutions and be fully equipped and empowered wherever they are.

See Him for Who He Truly Is

My husband and I were leading an encounter weekend, and a man and a woman from Iran came. They were around the age of twenty-five. During worship the man painted a picture. He said he felt so compelled to paint it but didn't know what it meant. He asked me what it meant, so I asked the Father to give me the interpretation of his painting. I told the man that his painting looked like a womb and something being reborn. He explained how part of the painting was all pink, making it look more like a womb, and he had made it black because he was not a fan of pink. Somehow my interpretation made sense to him. He told me he sensed an evil inside of him, but that he wanted to be free, to become new or reborn. He kept asking my husband and I questions, wanting to hear our story. As we told Him about Jesus in our own lives, he was at the edge of his seat, wanting to hear more.

A while later, my husband and I prayed for the woman who had come to the encounter weekend with the young man. We learned that someone had emotionally and physically abused her, an extremely traumatic experience that she chose not to share in great detail. My husband became vulnerable and shared about how he had learned to let go of unforgivingness toward people who had verbally and physically hurt him. After hearing how he became free, she chose to forgive those who had abused her. Huub and I led her through prayers of inner healing, inviting her to offer her pain to Jesus and ask what He would give in replacement for it.

As we were leading her to talk to Jesus, we encouraged her to speak in her own native tongue. However, when she did so, she wasn't able to hear anything. Later, we found out that when she would pray in her language, she was praying to Allah. She didn't hear anything when she asked Allah to speak to her, but when she asked Jesus, He spoke in a powerful way. She asked for the Holy

Spirit to come and fill her up, and she had a beautiful encounter. She told us she had always been cold, but when she asked the Holy Spirit into her life, she felt liquid, warm fire going through her veins.

Later that day, her friend came up to us to tell us how different his friend was since our time of prayer. With excitement he shared that he had known her for years, and she was suddenly completely different. He kept expressing how he wanted power and wisdom; he wanted our God. I told him how Jesus gave us wisdom and revelation; everything he had seen came from Jesus. He said, "No, I don't want Jesus. I don't want Jesus, I don't want Allah. I want your God!" I told him, "But Jesus is my God."

I realized that he lived in a devastating world of control. If he did not do what those in authority asked him to do, they would beat him, throw him in jail, or kill him. I saw the look on his face as he spoke, the fear and discomfort at sharing his true thoughts. The world he grew up in taught him what god looked like, and he didn't want to live in that world of control, devoted to a god he didn't know. Finally, he let us pray for him that he would see God (Jesus and the Father) for who He really is.

The world is longing to know Jesus for who He truly is. How will they know who He is unless we demonstrate it? How can we demonstrate it unless we've experienced it personally and continually? As we become full of who He is for us—extravagant love, goodness, encouragement, forgiveness, delight, and joy—we can then represent Him to others. Even when people have an encounter with the Father, they want the Father but don't want to be a part of church. We have an opportunity now to let go of everything we know in theory about what we've heard about Him and come to encounter who He truly is. Will you dare to ask Him to reveal

Himself to you? And as you so richly receive Him, you will freely give, unable to contain His goodness.

Precious, Valuable Ones

Jesus shared the parables of the lost sheep, the lost coin, and the lost son; each one is a parable about going out searching for what is lost. Jesus loved to meet the lost where they were. He was seen with sinners and tax collectors and often criticized by the Pharisees for his behavior, but he didn't care how He appeared to people. He went to the people who were the least lovely and the least reputable—the ones the world rejected. He seeks the lost, just as his parables demonstrate. The beauty of His stories is that they all end in rejoicing—a great feast and celebration. I'm convinced the Father and the host of heaven love to celebrate.

There is something valuable in each of the parables. However, I want to zoom in to the parable of the lost coin in order to reveal His heart for us.

Or suppose a woman has ten silver coins and loses one. Doesn't she light a lamp, sweep the house and search carefully until she finds it? And when she finds it, she calls her friends and neighbors together and says, "Rejoice with me; I have found my lost coin." In the same way, I tell you, there is rejoicing in the presence of the angels of God over one sinner who repents.

(Luke 15:8–10, NIV)

There are many symbols throughout this parable that I find very significant. A coin carries the image and superscription of the king under whose honor and authority it was issued. You were created in the image and likeness of the King of kings. His superscription marks you. His stamp of approval, identity, and authority are on you.

The woman in the parable only had ten silver coins, so when she lost one she felt it profoundly, just as a parent would feel the loss of a son or daughter who has walked away or is struggling with their identity. In order to help her in her search, she lit a lamp to cast light—or revelation—on her situation.

I would like to suggest that the woman was a glistening ray of hope for that one coin—that son or daughter who had forgotten who he or she was or lost the way. Using the light of God's revelation, she searched for them, sweeping up and removing all the stuff that would cover or hide them in the dirt. She separated the dirt from who they really are, calling them back to their true identity. Then they are revealed and restored to the revelation of who they truly are.

This parable of the coin reminded me of a time I was calling out to God as though He were far away. I was in my car, and I was looking for some money I had dropped. I needed it and I knew it was there, somewhere. I searched for it, having great confidence that I would find it. I felt like the Father said to me, "Search for me like this." I realized that He was inviting me to search for Him knowing that He was already there. At the time, I was just coming into an awareness of His presence and the continual connection we had.

As I was thinking about the parable of the woman and the pieces of silver, the revelation of what He told me in the car went even deeper in my heart. When He said, "Search for Me like this," I realized He also meant to search for Him in each and every person. He was inviting me to search for His thoughts and His love for people, search for a revelation of who they really are as precious, valuable, and loved sons and daughters of the King.

All of the symbols in the parable made sense to me: we are to shine the light of revelation over people, clean them off with love and truth, and call them back to who they really are. We are even to restore people to their identity with the stamp of approval and authority of the Father.

Let us look through everything that is unlovely, rejected, and outcast and search for Jesus in the midst of everything. That is what He demonstrated to us. He saw people differently, and now it is our turn to search and find the lost, who are made in His image. Ask the Lord if there is anyone in your life who needs to be found and revealed as a son or daughter of God. What does He like about that person and what are His dreams over his or her life? Let the search begin.

Don't Bury What You Carry
When you read Matthew 25:14–25, the parable of the talents, have you ever wondered what caused the one who received one talent to bury and hide what he was given? Jesus is our master who has entrusted and invested in us many gifts, talents, finances, and the kingdom of heaven. Our role is to bring the kingdom of heaven to the earth. We are to release and increase what He has invested in us in the same way the servants in the parable were meant to increase the wealth of the master.

In this parable, which Jesus likens to the kingdom of heaven, the master gave the servants money according to their ability. The ones who were entrusted with five and two talents immediately went out and doubled what the master gave them. However, the one who received one talent went and buried and hid what he was given. What kept him from immediately using what his master gave him to grow his master's wealth? What caused him to hide and bury the talent?

> After a long time the master of those servants returned and settled accounts with them. The man who had received five bags of gold brought the other five. "Master," he said, "you entrusted me with five bags of gold. See, I have gained five more." His master replied, "Well done, good and faithful servant! You have been faithful with a few things; I will put you in charge of many things. **Come and share your master's happiness!**"…Then the man who had received one bag of gold came. "Master," he said, "**I knew that you are a hard man**, harvesting where you have not sown and gathering where you have not scattered seed. **So I was afraid and went out and hid your gold in the ground.** See, here is what belongs to you."
>
> (Matt. 25:19–21 and 24–25, NIV)

Did you catch that? The servant who chose to bury the talent had a wrong image of the master. The other servants were commended and called good and faithful. The master rewarded them and put them in charge of many things. They also shared in the master's joy, joining him in celebration. Their perception and experience of the master was completely different from that of the servant with one talent. He saw his master as a harsh, stern, and hard man—a man without love who taxes men above their powers and doesn't give grace for any imperfect services. He depicted him as someone who enriches himself with others' toil, who gains where he did not labor.

When the servant told the master that he buried the one talent in the ground, his master asked why, if he was unwilling to take risks, he did not at least put the talent in a bank where it could have produced some increase. Just like the master, God's heart for you is that you wouldn't bury your gifts and talents but rather practice, in a safe way, investing what He has given you.

How do you see your heavenly Father? What causes you to bury or hide the gifts and talents the He has invested in you? Do you see Him for who He really is, or do you perceive Him to be something else entirely? He is a good and loving Father who doesn't require more than what you are able to give. As your ability increases, He is waiting to make you a ruler over much. When you take risks, he wants to celebrate with you and invite you into His joy.

His Glory Will Appear Upon You

When you see darkness in the world, what effect does it have on you? Do you rise up or shrink back? Have you ever wondered why God doesn't just do something about it? In Exodus 3, the Lord tells Moses that He has seen the misery of His people in Egypt, that He hears their cries caused by the slave drivers and shares in their suffering. The Lord said that He was coming to rescue them. So why didn't God do it alone? Just like He used Moses, He uses you and me to deliver His people. He has heard their cry; will we go out and deliver them? In terrible times so many people look to God, wondering why He hasn't rescued people. He can and He has. However, He uses you; He uses me.

> For behold, darkness will cover the earth And deep darkness the peoples; **But** the LORD will rise upon you And **His glory will appear upon you.**

> (Isa. 60:2, NASB)

His glory has risen upon you and will be seen in you. You can operate in every supernatural realm in which Jesus operated. He is our model as we learn to walk as a son or daughter of God. Like Moses, we might feel insecure when we are stepping out with such great ambition. We can choose to look at our insecurities and ourselves, or we can step into what God has intended for us. We can also practice behind the scenes like Moses did. He didn't go directly to Pharaoh, commanding the release of the people. Moses threw down his staff in private before he ever stood in front of Pharaoh. We need to practice healing, signs, wonders, miracles, words of knowledge, and prophetic words before we go out. When we are ready, we can show off our God to be the strongest and most powerful.

When Moses's staff was thrown down in front of Pharoah, it turned into a snake. However, all Pharaoh's wise men and sorcerers and the Egyptian magicians could do the same thing. That is until Moses's staff ate up all of the others. As His sons and daughters, we have a great invitation to demonstrate that our God is the most powerful God. For too long the church has been hiding within their walls, when we need to arise and shine instead. God has invited us to partner with Him. However, partnering with Him requires you to step outside of your comfort zone and stretch out your hand to heal the sick. Remember, God wants to deliver His people, and He uses you to do it.

A Glorious Beacon

In that night God appeared to Solomon and said to him, "Ask what I shall give you." Solomon said to God, "You have dealt with my father David with great loving kindness, and have made me king in his place. Now, O LORD God, Your promise to my father David is fulfilled, for You have made me king over a people as numerous as the dust of the earth. **Give me now wisdom and knowledge, that I may go out and come in before this people,** for who can rule this great people of Yours?"

(2 Chron. 1:7–10, NASB)

God placed Solomon as the ruler after David, and Solomon earnestly desired to have wisdom and knowledge to lead his people. Solomon asked God for wisdom of how to deal with the affairs of his people, how to govern the people near and far. He positioned himself to be like a shepherd, safeguarding his flock, his kingdom (Num. 27:17). He desired to rule His people in such a beautiful way—not wanting to leave them to wander without guidance and protection like sheep without a shepherd.

The type of discernment Solomon was asking for was not natural human judgment on how to see and make decisions, but wisdom and knowledge that looks beyond what human judgment can bring or see. He desired to distinguish between what is true and false in situations without prejudice and to pass the correct sentence sitting as a judge on behalf of the people. He wanted to rule his kingdom with truth and righteousness, which greatly benefited the people. The wisdom he asked for and carried was evident in his life and had a great impact (1 Kings 3:16–28).

God said to Solomon, "Because you had this in mind, and did not ask for riches, wealth or honor, or the life of those who hate you, nor have you even asked for long life, but you have asked for yourself wisdom and knowledge that you may rule My people over whom I have made you king, wisdom and knowledge have been granted to you. And I will give you riches and wealth and honor, such as none of the kings who were before you has possessed nor those who will come after you."

(2 Chron. 1:11–12, NASB)

Solomon was not focused on what would benefit him, but rather on what would benefit the people in his kingdom. This pleased God, so the Father set him up for even more success. Not only did He give him wisdom and knowledge but God gave him great wealth and honor. I believe it was meant to be a beacon, a visual display, drawing people to come and see what it looks like when God is with you.

When the queen of Sheba heard about the **fame of Solomon and his relationship to the Lord,** she came to test Solomon with hard questions. Arriving at Jerusalem with a very great caravan—with camels carrying spices, large quantities of gold, and precious stones—she came to Solomon and talked with him about all that she had on her mind. Solomon answered all her questions; nothing was too hard for the king to explain to her. When the queen of Sheba saw all the wisdom of Solomon and the palace he had built, the food on his table, the seating of his officials, the attending servants in their robes, his cupbearers, and the burnt offerings he made at the temple of the Lord, she was overwhelmed.

She said to the king, "The report I heard in my own country about your achievements and your wisdom is true. But I did not believe these things until I came and saw with my own eyes. Indeed, not even half was told me; in wisdom and wealth you have far exceeded the report I heard. **How happy your people must be! How happy your officials, who continually stand before you and hear your wisdom! Praise be to the Lord your God,** who has delighted in you and placed you on the throne of Israel. **Because of**

the Lord's eternal love for Israel, he has made you king to maintain justice and righteousness."

(1 Kings 10:1–9, NIV)

The queen of Sheba was drawn to Solomon by what she heard regarding his relationship with the Lord and what that looked like. God gave great wealth and honor to Solomon, which served as an invitation for people to come see a visual display of His glory. The queen of Sheba was overwhelmed with what she experienced. She saw the way Solomon shepherded his people, how he lived his life and treated those who served him. She said, "How happy your people must be!" And she praised the Lord. This encounter with Solomon revealed to her a God who loved His people well by setting over them a leader who in wisdom would maintain justice and righteousness.

Like Solomon, the Father has placed you in a kingdom, a realm of influence. If you ask for wisdom, He will give it to you without measure, for the benefit of the people around you (James 1:5). God didn't only give Solomon wisdom and knowledge but also blessed him with riches, wealth, and honor. Let it also be for us that as we serve God's people, we become more and more like a shining beacon, a visual display for people to encounter what it looks like to have a relationship with God.

Nations will come to your light,
and kings to the brightness of your dawn.
Lift up your eyes and look about you:
All assemble and come to you;
your sons come from afar,
and your daughters are carried on the hip.
Then you will look and be radiant,

your heart will throb and swell with joy.

(Isa. 60:3–5, NIV)

As we arise and shine, revealing who the Father is and what it looks like to live in relationship and connection with Him, nations and kings will see us as a brilliant, shining light, like a beacon in a dark world. We will be like a beacon, calling His sons and daughters home to His heart. His sons and daughters are flocking from all around the world to come home, to have an encounter with who He is. And we will be overflowing with joy and delight at the sight of it!

And all from Sheba will come,
bearing gold and incense
and **proclaiming the praise of the Lord.**

(Isa. 60:6, NIV)

The same will happen for us as it did for Solomon: that kings, leaders, and people will come and taste who the Father is through us. "How happy your people must be!" As they encounter who He is and see He is real and true, they will desire the same relationship with the Father that you are revealing to them. This is the greatest movement; it is here and is ever increasing.

Dreaming with God: Receiving Wisdom and Revelation
Dream with God and position yourself in a place to serve your "kingdom" and the people around you just as Solomon did. As you dream over your area of influence, ask God to give you wisdom, understanding, knowledge, revelation, solutions, and creative ideas that would benefit the people you come into contact with. What would your family look like? What would your church look

like? What would your business look like? What would your city look like?

He is calling you to arise and shine in dark places, and He lives in you and has clothed Himself with you. You are His hands and feet, His extended arms. He has given you everything you need to have the greatest impact. Do not shrink back when darkness comes, but arise, shine, and be confident in who you are and who He is in you. Shine even brighter because your God is with you and has made His home in you.

Every day you are given divine appointments. These appointments are the people you come into contact with. Let the measuring stick for your success be the question, "Did I love the one in front of me?" Did you see them? Did you live in the moment and follow the way of love in releasing spiritual gifts? God will be seen in you as He gives you everything you need to serve His kingdom where He has positioned you.

This is the greatest movement that is here and is ever increasing—you and all of His sons and daughters arising, shining, and being revealed. This movement is you discovering what unique gifts and talents you carry. It is you shining brilliantly with the glory you carry inside of you. As we arise, we become revealers of the knowledge of the glory of God, revealing who He is and shining bright like glorious beacons, calling people out of the darkness to come home into the Father's heart.

As you represent the Father, stand, shine, and present yourself to the world. You have this one life. What will you truly live for? The earth is waiting and groaning for you to be revealed. The ones you are going to reach are waiting for you. What will you dream with the Father and release on the earth? Will you decide to cheat death and live beyond your own life, releasing what you carry to the next generation? What will your life on this earth mark history with? Come alive and fully live! Arise, shine, and be revealed (Isa. 60:1). You are part of the greatest movement, and together we will fill the earth with the knowledge of the glory of the Lord (Hab. 2:14).

Made in the USA
Middletown, DE
18 September 2017